D0338736

HDRAWN

Automobile Power Accessories

Automobile

CHILTON'S AUTOMOBILE MECHANICS' SERIES

Under the Advisory Editorship of Harold S. Bostwick
Coordinator, Murrell Dobbins Vocational-Technical School, Philadelphia

Power
Accessories

HAROLD T. GLENN

Member, Society of Automotive Engineers; Instructor in the Public School System, Long Beach, California; Author, "Automobile Engine Rebuilding and Maintenance," "How to Locate Automobile Troubles," "Exploring Automechanics," "Youth at the Wheel," and "Safe Living"

CHILTON COMPANY—BOOK DIVISION
Publishers—*Philadelphia & New York*

FIRST EDITION

COPYRIGHT © 1959 BY
HAROLD T. GLENN

All Rights Reserved

Published in Philadelphia by Chilton Company
and simultaneously in Toronto, Canada, by Ambassador Books, Ltd.

LIBRARY OF CONGRESS CATALOG CARD NUMBER 59–9641

MANUFACTURED IN THE UNITED STATES OF AMERICA
BY QUINN & BODEN COMPANY, INC., RAHWAY, N. J.

Chilton's Automotive Library

Automobile Chassis Design

Automobile Electrical Equipment

Automobile Repair Manual

The Automotive Chassis (Without Powerplant)

Battery Chargers and Charging

Class Progress Chart

Diesel Maintenance

Group Assignment Chart

Handbook of Automotive Shop Kinks

High-Speed Combustion Engines

High-Speed Diesel Engines

Individual Progress Chart

The Modern Diesel

The Motor Vehicle

The Practical Pedagogue

Torque Converters or Transmissions

Chilton's Automobile Mechanics' Series

Automatic Transmission

The Automobile Chassis

The Automobile Electrical System

The Automobile Engine

Automobile Engine Rebuilding and Maintenance

Automobile Power Accessories

The Automobile Transmission and Drive Line

The Automotive Machine Shop

Automotive Tools

Body and Fender Repair and Refinishing

Chilton's Automotive Job Sheets

I. The Engine, with supplement on The Fuel System

II. The Chassis

III. The Automotive Electrical System

Teachers' Manual and Source-book

196782

Foreword

This book is the third in Chilton's Automobile Mechanics' Series, developed to satisfy the demand by educators and industry for better textbooks. No expense has been spared to make this Series outstanding.

The authors of the Series have been selected for both their teaching and their writing ability. Each one is actively engaged either in teaching or in work closely allied to shop instruction in the automotive field. Besides drawing on their collective background, they have consulted experienced men in educational systems throughout the country and in the automotive service industry to determine the Series' content, organization, and method of presentation. The material assembled from this effort was further studied and discussed in conferences with members of Chilton's Technical Education Advisory Board.

It should be mentioned that the Series follows the course laid out by the Automotive Industry-Vocational Education Conference on Public School Automotive Instruction. This body recently recommended that publishers in vocational-technical education utilize the "combined thinking of educators and automotive service specialists throughout the country." We believe that this Series meets the aims of this important Conference.

The Series has been specifically designed to serve the needs of both students and teachers. Modern and new in every respect, it is written in clear language, is profusely illustrated, and is complete in its coverage.

By making this new material available to American vocational-technical educators, we hope that they will be better able to prepare their students for a more satisfying career in automotive repair and maintenance. We also hope that the students, when they eventually become associated with the automotive industry, will be able to offer even more effective service to American automobile owners.

HAROLD S. BOSTWICK,
Consulting Editor

Preface

Automobile Power Accessories is a book designed to meet the needs of the progressive mechanic in keeping abreast of modern technological developments. It is written in simplified form so that it can be used in the training of students and apprentices. Teachers of automechanics will find it a valuable teaching tool.

The book is profusely illustrated. In some cases, especially where the overhaul directions of complex equipment are being discussed, detailed graphic instructions are given, each step being illustrated by an action-type picture. In most cases, the instructions are preceded by an exploded view for the mechanic to be able to visualize the relationships of the various parts.

The questions at the end of each chapter are carefully worded to conform to, and closely follow the sequence of, the text so that the book can be used as a workbook.

THE AUTHOR

Acknowledgments

The author wishes to express his sincere appreciation to the following contributors who so graciously supplied the illustrative material:

Allstadt Manufacturing Company—Figs. 254, 263

American Motors Sales Corporation—Figs. 245, 257, 264

Bendix Products Division, Bendix Aviation Corporation—Figs. 77–92

Buick Motor Division, General Motors Corporation—Figs. 117, 119, 120, 122–128, 130–134, 137, 139, 140, 142, 146, 152, 158–160, 247, 248, 249, 251, 271, 272, 274

Cadillac Motor Car Division, General Motors Corporation—Figs. 116, 121, 135, 136, 138, 141, 143, 145, 148–151, 153, 156, 157, 161, 162

Chevrolet Motor Division, General Motors Corporation—Figs. 31, 32, 34, 35, 40, 41, 273, 275

Chrysler Division, Chrysler Corporation—Figs. 96–99, 101–113, 115, 191, 199, 224, 226, 229, 278, 279

DeSoto Division, Chrysler Corporation—Figs. 1–3, 7–17, 19–25, 202–206, 235–244, 260–262, 276

Dodge Division, Chrysler Corporation—Figs. 4–6, 44, 46, 47, 51–55, 268–270, 277

Edsel Division, Ford Motor Company—Figs. 219, 220, 230–234

Ford Division, Ford Motor Company—Figs. 165–190, 193–198, 217, 218

Lincoln Division, Ford Motor Company—Figs. 200, 201, 222, 223, 225

M-E-L Division, Ford Motor Company—Figs. 246, 253, 255, 256, 258, 259, 265

Mercury Division, Ford Motor Company—Figs. 26–30, 33, 36–39, 43, 69, 73–76, 207–216, 221, 227, 228, 250, 252

Plymouth Division, Chrysler Corporation—Figs. 18, 42, 45, 48–50, 56–68, 70, 71, 93–95, 100, 114, 192, 266, 267

Pontiac Motor Division, General Motors Corporation—Figs. 72, 118, 129, 144, 147, 154, 155, 163, 164

Especial thanks are due to my wife, Anna, for her assistance in revising and proofreading.

HAROLD T. GLENN

Contents

Automobile Power Accessories

1

POWER STEERING

Power steering uses hydraulic pressure built up by an engine-operated pump to assist the driver in turning the front wheels. In all power-steering designs, driver "feel" is built into the system by having the driver do some of the work. Two types of power-steering mechanisms are in common use—a power-assist linkage and a power-assist piston operating within the steering gear box. The latter is known as a coaxial unit.

In each case, movement of the steering wheel causes movement of a valve which directs oil, under pressure, to a piston to help the driver turn the front wheels. The valve mechanism is designed so that, the more pressure the driver applies, the more hydraulic pressure is applied to the power-assist piston.

The hydraulic valve mechanism is designed to be uni-directional—that is, power assists the driver in turning the front wheels, but road shocks are opposed by hydraulic pressure, and, therefore, are not transmitted back to the steering wheel.

Several types of hydraulic pumps are used: sleeve, vane, roller, rotor, and slipper. Each contains a pressure-relief valve to maintain uniform operating pressures within the system. Each has a reservoir to store the Automatic Transmission Type "A" fluid which is used in every system.

The following service procedures describe the disassembly and assembly of a coaxial type of power-steering unit, a type used on late-model Chrysler products, and a linkage-type unit used on Ford products. These two units are representative of all others commonly in use.

Because most hydraulic pumps are constructed along similar lines, it is possible to cover them all by detailing the service procedures of two common types: the sleeve and the vane. The added cut-away drawings show the variations of the other types.

COAXIAL POWER STEERING

Description. All parts of the power unit are fitted into an elongated tubular-shaped housing concentrically located about the steering

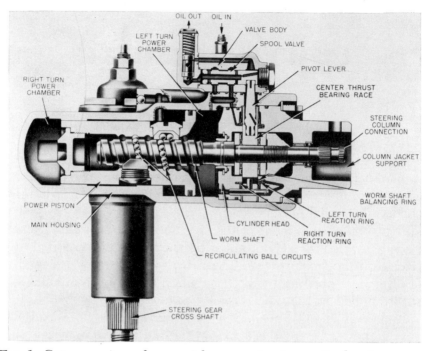

FIG. 1. Cutaway view of a coaxial power steering unit, showing names and placement of main parts.

FIG. 2. Cutaway view of power piston and sector gear.

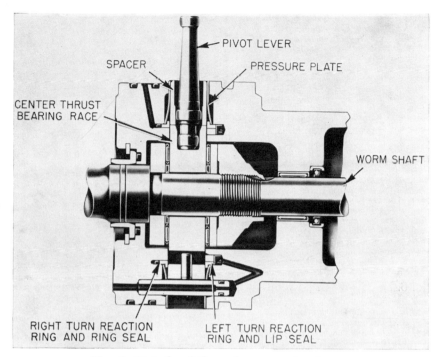

FIG. 3. Details of the valve actuating lever.

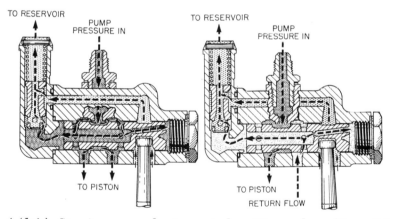

FIG. 4 (*left*). Steering gear valve in *neutral* position and resulting oil flow.

FIG. 5 (*right*). Steering gear valve in *left-turn* position and resulting oil flow.

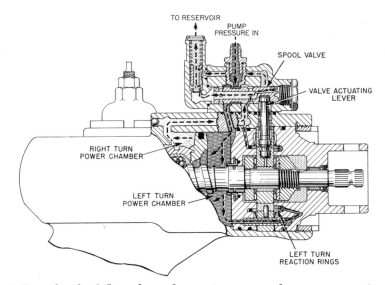

FIG. 6. Details of oil flow through steering gear valve to power piston in *left-turn* position.

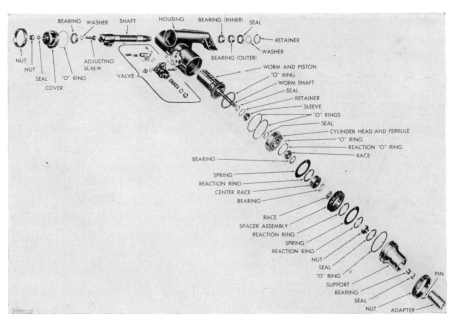

FIG. 7. Exploded view of coaxial-type power steering unit.

gear column. Basically, the unit consists of two parts, a worm and a rack. The rack meshes with the sector gear and is, also, the power-assist piston.

The worm acts in a manner similar to a bolt and nut; rotation of the worm causes its shaft to move axially a few thousandths of an inch. This moves a valve which directs oil, under pressure, to the piston to assist the driver in turning the steering wheel.

Theory of Operation:

Straight-Ahead Position. With the steering valve in the *neutral* position (center), oil flows through both of the grooves equally because the two lands of the valve are centered in the grooves of the valve body. The oil reaches both sides of the power piston with equal pressure and so no movement results.

Turns. When the driver makes a left turn, for example, the worm shaft moves to the left (a few thousandths of an inch), moving the center thrust bearing race with it. This movement tips the pilot lever which moves the spool valve to the left. This directs oil, under pressure, to the left-turn power chamber (right side of the piston) and pushes the piston to the left to actuate the steering linkage of the front wheels.

In the reaction area, oil is directed, from the left-turn power chamber, to the left-turn reaction ring which tries to straighten out the pivot lever and return it to a neutral position. As soon as the driver releases pressure on the steering wheel, the center thrust bearing race, and the pivot lever, are returned to neutral by pressure on the left-turn reaction ring. Equal oil pressure is then directed to both sides of the piston.

The restraining force of the reaction spring must be overcome by driver effort before the center race can move. This contributes to driver "feel."

Service Procedures:

Disassembling. (Each of the following steps is illustrated. The number in the lower right-hand corner of the illustration agrees with the numbered steps below.)

1. Drain the steering gear through the pressure and return connections by turning the steering tube coupling from one end of its travel to the other. Remove the coupling pin. It must be supported as shown to avoid damaging the bearings.

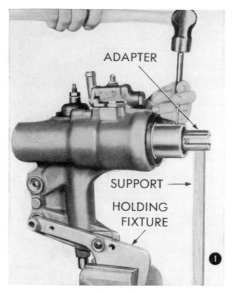

ADAPTER

SUPPORT →

HOLDING
FIXTURE

Fig. 8

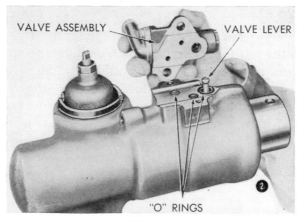

VALVE ASSEMBLY   VALVE LEVER

"O" RINGS

Fig. 9

2. Remove the valve body housing attaching screws and remove the valve body and three "O" rings.

3. Remove the valve lever by prying under the spherical head. Do not use pliers; otherwise, you may collapse the slotted end of the valve lever and destroy the critical clearance of the spherical head.

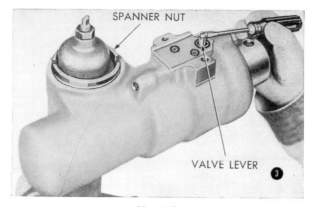

Fig. 10

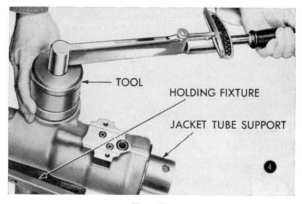

Fig. 11

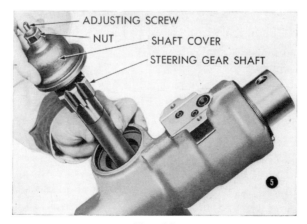

Fig. 12

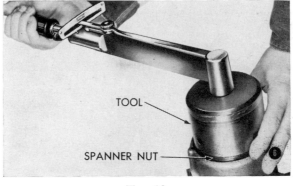

F̅ɪɢ. 13

4. Loosen the gear shaft adjusting screw locknut and remove the gear shaft cover nut.

5. To remove the gear shaft and cover as an assembly, rotate the worm shaft to its full-right position. Then return it to the center of its travel and lift it straight out.

6. Remove the steering column support nut and the tanged washer.

7. To remove the power train, turn the worm shaft to its full-right position, and then back it off as much as necessary to align the holes in the column and worm shaft. Insert a drift through the holes to keep the parts from turning as you carefully withdraw the assembly.

8. Remove the worm shaft upper oil seal.

9. Remove the reaction seal from its groove in the face of the jacket support by blowing air into the ferrule chamber. Remove the large "O" ring from its groove.

10. Remove the two "O" rings in the two outer grooves in the cylinder head. Then use air pressure to blow into the oil hole located in the groove between the two "O" ring grooves to remove the lower reaction "O" ring.

11. To disassemble the control valve, compress the pressure control valve spring and remove the spring retainer pin, the spring, and the pressure control valve piston. Remove the two screws attaching the pressure control valve body to the steering valve and remove the valve body. Carefully shake out the valve piston. Do not remove the valve end plug unless it leaks.

12. To remove the gear shaft oil seal, remove the snap ring and then attach a puller to remove the seal.

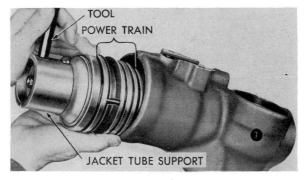

Fig. 14

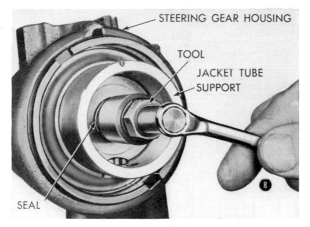

Fig. 15

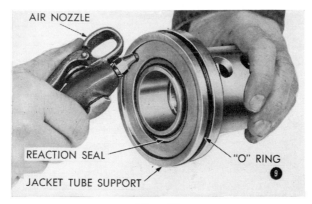

Fig. 16

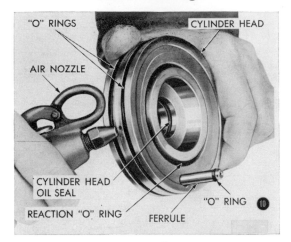

Fɪɢ. 17

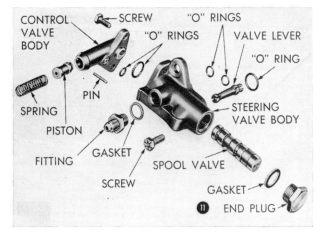

Fɪɢ. 18

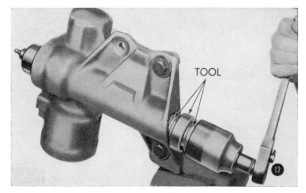

Fɪɢ. 19

Cleaning and Inspecting. Clean all parts in solvent and blow dry. Parts should be inspected for wear, nicks, and burrs. Replace all "O" rings and seals.

Assembling. (In general, the assembly is the reverse of disassembly, therefore, only the especially important steps are illustrated.)

13. To assemble the power train, slide the cylinder head over the worm shaft. Lubricate and install the following parts in the order listed: lower thrust bearing race (thick), lower thrust bearing,

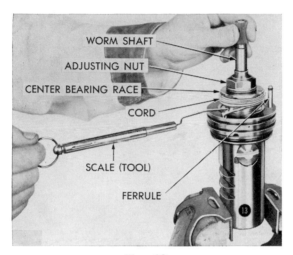

WORM SHAFT

ADJUSTING NUT

CENTER BEARING RACE

CORD

SCALE (TOOL)

FERRULE

Fig. 20

lower reaction spring over the ferrule, lower reaction ring (with flange *up* so that the ring protrudes through the reaction spring), and the center bearing race (index the control lever hole with the hole in the center of the bearing race). Then install the outer spacer, upper thrust bearing, upper thrust bearing race (thin), and a new worm shaft thrust bearing nut. Tighten the nut as follows: turn the worm shaft counterclockwise one-half turn and hold the worm shaft while tightening the nut to 10 foot-pounds torque.

Rotate the worm center bearing race several turns to position all parts, and then loosen the adjusting nut. Retighten the worm bearing adjusting nut once more to give a bearing torque of 8 to 16 ounces. To check this torque, place several rounds of cord around the center bearing race. Make a loop in the end of the cord into which you can hook a breaker arm spring scale. Pulling on the cord will cause the bearing race to rotate. If the adjusting nut is tightened properly, the scale reading should be between 8 and 16 ounces.

14. Depress the flange of the adjusting nut into the depression in the worm shaft to lock it securely. It is important to recheck the torque reading at this time to be sure that it has not changed through locking.

15. Install the center bearing spacer over the center bearing race to engage the dowel pin with the slot in the center bearing race. Place the inner and outer reaction rings over the center spacer and install the upper reaction spring with the cylinder head ferrule

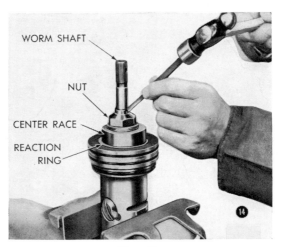

WORM SHAFT

NUT

CENTER RACE

REACTION
RING

Fig. 21

through the hole in the spring. Install a new "O" ring in the ferrule groove.

Lubricate the small bore of the column jacket support and install the support over the worm shaft while carefully engaging the cylinder head ferrule and the "O" ring. Make sure that the reaction rings enter their grooves in the jacket support.

16. To install the power train assembly, align the parts so that the valve lever hole in the center bearing spacer is 90° counterclockwise from the piston rack teeth. Lock all parts by entering a drift through the jacket support and worm shaft holes. Lubricate the bore of the housing and carefully install the power train assembly. To protect the "O" rings, cover the aligning notch in the steering gear housing with an 0.0015" feeler gauge blade. Be sure that the valve lever hole is in the *up* position to line up with the control valve lever clearance hole. Align the valve lever holes with the aligning tool.

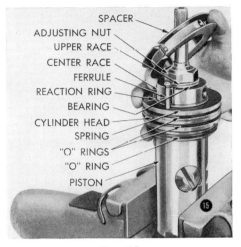

SPACER
ADJUSTING NUT
UPPER RACE
CENTER RACE
FERRULE
REACTION RING
BEARING
CYLINDER HEAD
SPRING
"O" RINGS
"O" RING
PISTON

Fig. 22

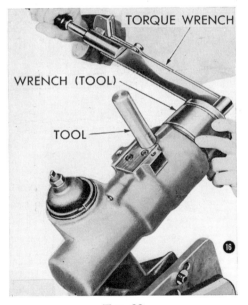

TORQUE WRENCH
WRENCH (TOOL)
TOOL

Fig. 23

Install the column support spanner nut and tighten it to 150 foot-pounds torque. Adjust the piston to the center of its travel and install the gear shaft and cover assembly so that the sector teeth index with the piston rack teeth. Make sure that the "O" ring is positioned

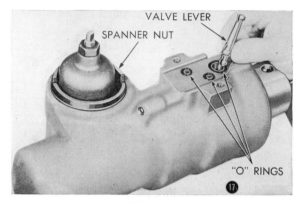

Fig. 24

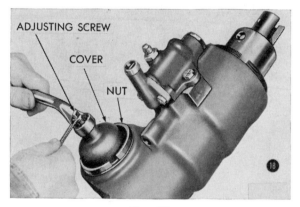

Fig. 25

in the face of the cover. Install the cover spanner nut and tighten it to 100 foot-pounds torque.

17. Remove the aligning tool and install the valve lever (double bearing end first) into the center bearing spacer through the hole in the steering housing so that the slots in the valve lever are parallel to the worm shaft in order to engage the anti-rotation pin in the center bearing race. Install the valve body on the housing, making sure that the valve lever enters the hole in the piston. Be sure that the "O" ring seals are in place and tighten the valve mounting screws to 30 inch-pounds torque.

Adjusting:

18. Adjust the gear shaft backlash by loosening the adjusting screw until backlash is evident. Then retighten the adjusting screw until the backlash just disappears. Continue tightening the screw for ⅜ to ½ turn more, and then tighten the locknut to 50 foot-pounds torque.

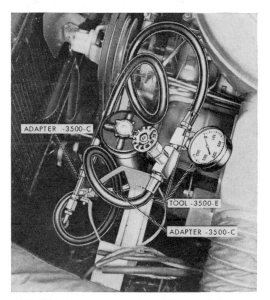

FIG. 26. Hooking up gauges for troubleshooting.

Position the valve body on the housing so that equal pressure is applied to the power-assist piston for turns in each direction. To do this, connect the test gauges between the steering gear housing and the pump. Start the engine to apply pressure to the unit. Lightly tap on one of the pressure control valve screws or on the valve end plug until the setting gives equal gauge readings when the gear shaft is turned slowly in each direction. After the valve body is located correctly, tighten the attaching screws to 15 foot-pounds torque.

TROUBLESHOOTING

TROUBLES	CAUSES

1. Hard steering

1a. Tires not properly inflated.

1b. Low oil level (usually accompanied by pump noises).

1c. Loose pump belt.

1d. Oil on pump belt.

1e. Steering linkage needs lubrication.

1f. Power steering pump output low.

1g. Steering gear malfunctions:
  (1) Cross shaft adjustment too tight.
  (2) Pressure control valve stuck in closed position.
  (3) External oil leakage at the following points: Lower sector shaft oil seal, Sector shaft adjusting screw seal, Sector shaft cover "O" ring seal, and Valve housing-to-gear housing "O" rings.
  (4) Defective or damaged valve lever. If the pressure gauge will build up to 850 to 950 psi, check the following points: defective or damaged gear shaft bearings; dirt or chips in the steering gear; damaged column support worm shaft bearings; damaged thrust bearing or excessive preload adjustment; or a rough, hard-to-turn worm and piston assembly.
  (5) Excessive internal leakage. If the pressure gauge will not build up to 850 to 950 psi, check the following points: cylinder head "O" rings; cylinder head reaction seal; cylinder head worm shaft oil seal assem-

TROUBLESHOOTING—(Continued)

TROUBLES   CAUSES

bly; column support-to-ferrule "O" ring seal; column support reaction seal; and the cylinder head "O" rings.

2. Poor recovery from turns

2a. Tires not properly inflated.
2b. Steering linkage binding.
2c. Improper wheel alignment.
2d. Damaged or defective steering tube bearing.
2e. Steering wheel column jacket and steering unit not properly aligned.
2f. Steering gear malfunctions:
   (1) Improper cross shaft mesh adjustment.
   (2) Pressure control valve piston stuck in *open* position.
   (3) Column support spanner nut loose.
   (4) Defective or damaged valve lever
   (5) Improper worm thrust bearing adjustment.
   (6) Burrs or nicks in reaction ring grooves in cylinder head.
   (7) Defective or damaged cylinder head worm shaft seal ring.
   (8) Dirt or chips in steering gear unit.
   (9) Rough or catchy worm and piston assembly.

3. Temporary increase in effort when turning steering wheel

3a. Low oil level.
3b. Loose pump belt.
3c. Oil on pump belt.
3d. Binding steering linkage.
3e. Engine idled too slow.
3f. Defective power steering pump.
3g. Air in system. (Work steering wheel from right to left until air is expelled.)

TROUBLESHOOTING—(Continued)

TROUBLES	CAUSES
	3h. Gear malfunctions: (1) External leakage. (2) Improper cross shaft adjustment. (3) Excessive internal leakage.
4. Excessive steering wheel freeplay	4a. Improper cross shaft adjustment. 4b. Column support spanner nut loose. 4c. Improper worm thrust bearing adjustment.
5. Lack of assistance—one direction	5a. Oil leaking past worm shaft cast iron oil seal ring or ferrule "O" ring.
6. Lack of assistance—both directions	6a. Broken "D" ring on worm piston. 6b. Piston end plug loose. 6c. Reaction seal missing. 6d. Pump belt slipping. 6e. Pump output low.
7. Noises	7a. Buzzing noise in neutral, stops when steering wheel is turned —sticking pressure control valve. 7b. Noisy power pump. 7c. Damaged hydraulic lines. 7d. Pressure control valve sticking. 7e. Improper sector shaft mesh adjustment. 7f. Air in system.
8. Self-steering—or leads to one side	8a. Tires not properly inflated. 8b. Improper wheel alignment. 8c. Steering wheel off-center when car is traveling straight ahead. 8d. Valve body out of adjustment: (1) Steering to the left—Move steering valve housing *down* on steering housing. (2) Steering to the right—Move steering valve housing *up* on steering housing. 8e. Valve lever damaged. 8f. Column support spanner nut loose.

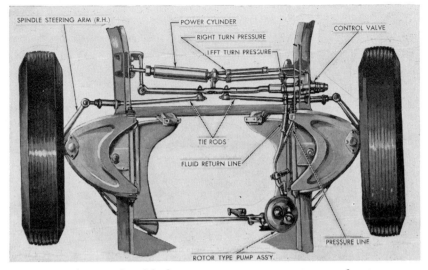

FIG. 27. Details of linkage-type power steering mechanism.

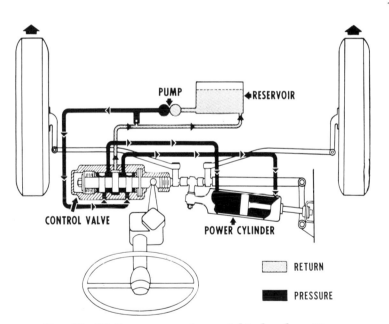

FIG. 28. Oil flow pattern in *straight-ahead* position.

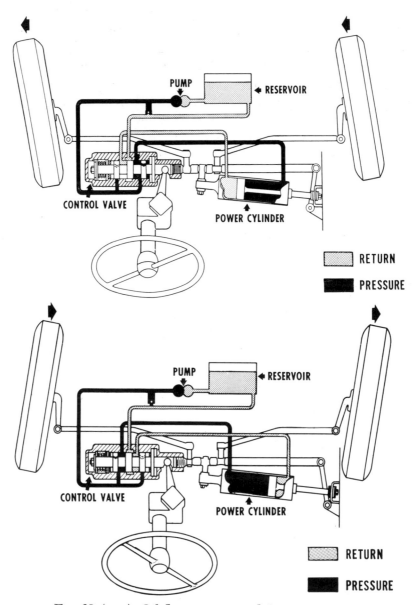

Fɪɢ. 29 (*top*). Oil flow pattern in *left-turn* position.

Fɪɢ. 30 (*bottom*). Oil flow pattern in *right-turn* position.

POWER-ASSIST, LINKAGE-TYPE STEERING

Description. The linkage type of power steering includes a power cylinder which actuates the steering linkage. Within the power cylinder is a control valve which directs oil to either side of the power-assist piston, depending on which turn is being made. The system contains a belt-driven pump to develop hydraulic pressure.

The pump draws oil from the reservoir and builds up pressure to operate the system. Within the pump is a pressure-relief valve which governs the system pressures according to the varying conditions of operation.

Theory of Operation:

Straight-Ahead Position. When the front wheels are in the straight-ahead position, the control valve spool is held in the *neutral* position (center) by its centering spring. The fluid flows around the valve lands and is directed with equal pressure to both sides of the power piston so no movement results.

Turns. When the driver exerts about 4-pounds pressure to the steering wheel for a left turn, for example, the valve spool overcomes the pressure of the centering spring and moves toward the right-hand end of the valve. This directs oil, under pressure, to the right side of the power cylinder, and the rear of the wheels move to the right. The fluid, trapped in the left side of the power cylinder, is by-passed back to the reservoir.

When the driver releases pressure on the steering wheel, the valve spool centering spring forces the spool back to its *neutral* position (center) and balanced forces on both sides of the power cylinder piston result. In the absence of a positive operating pressure, the front wheels tend to return to the straight-ahead position as a normal effect of front-wheel alignment.

Service Procedures. (Each of the following steps is illustrated. The number in the lower right-hand corner of the illustration agrees with the numbered steps below.)

Disassembling:

Removing the Control Valve from the Car:

1. To remove the control valve, loosen the tie rod-to-control valve clamp (4), disconnect the two pump-to-control valve hose connec-

Fig. 31

Fig. 32

tions (1 & 2), and allow the fluid to drain. Disconnect the two remaining valve-to-power cylinder hoses.

2. Remove the retaining nut from the ball stud to the pitman arm connection and disconnect the control valve from the pitman arm. Turn the pitman arm to the right to clear the control valve and unscrew the valve from the relay rod.

Disassembling the Control Valve:

3. Remove the dust cover, the retaining pin, and the nut from the end of the valve shaft. Remove the two retaining bolts connecting the valve assembly housing to the adapter assembly housing. Separate the two assemblies.

Fig. 33

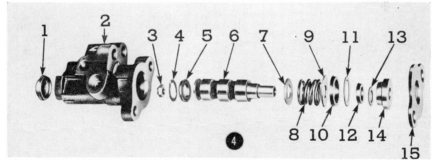

Fig. 34

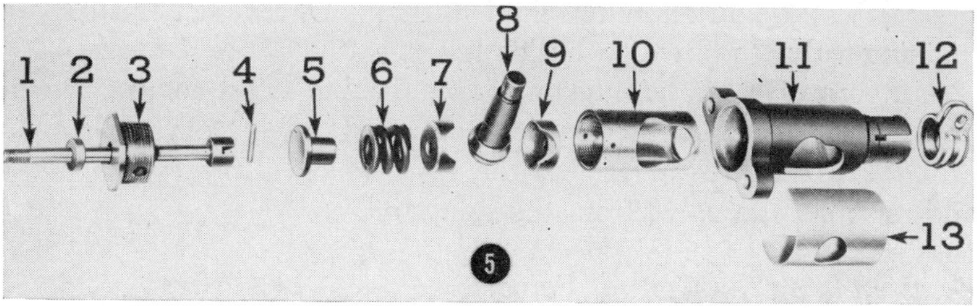

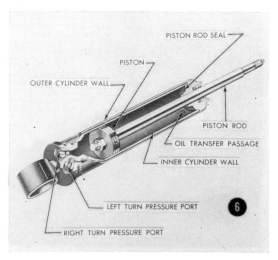

FIG. 35

4. Disassemble the various parts making up the control valve assembly: (1) dust shield, (2) housing, (3) nut, (4) washer, (5) seal, (6) valve spool, (7) washer, (8) spring, (9) washer, (10) seal, (11) washer, (12) seal, (13) washer, (14) vee seal block, and (15) spacer.

5. To disassemble the control valve adapter assembly, remove the ball stud cover (13) from the adapter assembly housing (11). Push the ball stud (8) to the end of the adapter housing and remove the lock pin (4). Remove the threaded ball plug adjuster (3) and the valve shaft (1). Remove the ball seat plug (5) and spring (6). Remove the ball seats (7 & 9) and the ball stud (8). Remove the bearing sleeve (10).

6. The construction of the power cylinder assembly does not permit the repair or replacement of internal parts. If the unit is worn or leaks, replace it with a new assembly.

PISTON ROD SEAL

PISTON

OUTER CYLINDER WALL

PISTON ROD

OIL TRANSFER PASSAGE

INNER CYLINDER WALL

LEFT TURN PRESSURE PORT

RIGHT TURN PRESSURE PORT

FIG. 36

Cleaning and Inspecting. Wash all metal parts in solvent and dry them with a lint-free cloth. Inspect all parts for wear or scratches. Test the spool valve fit in the housing; it should drop freely of its own weight. Replace all worn parts, seals, and gaskets.

FIG. 37

FIG. 38

Assembling. (In general, the assembly is the reverse of disassembly, therefore, only the especially important steps are illustrated.)

7. Assemble the control valve and the control valve assemblies.

8. Tighten the valve shaft adjusting nut securely. Then loosen it, not over a quarter turn, until the lock pin can be inserted. Move the ball stud back and forth in the sleeve slot to check the spool free movement. It should move about 0.060″ in each direction from center. Install the centering spring cap and tighten the two bolts to 4 to 6 foot-pounds torque.

9. Install a nut on the ball stud so that it can be placed in a vise to check the valve spool for free movement. Push on the end of the sleeve to feel the free play.

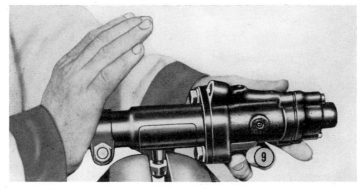

Fig. 39

Installing on Car:

10. Install the control valve on the relay rod so that the distance from the center of the control valve ball stud to the center of the

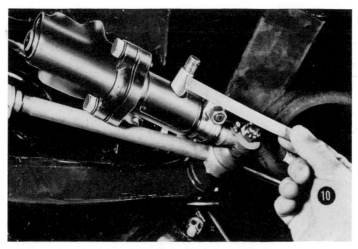

Fig. 40

tie rod end ball stud is according to the car manufacturer's specifications. Tighten and secure the clamp.

11. Install the power cylinder. Reconnect the hoses and fill the system with Type "A" fluid. Bleed the air by raising the front end of the car, running the engine at 1500 rpm, and turning the steering wheel once each way until it contacts each stop.

Fig. 41

TROUBLESHOOTING

TROUBLES	CAUSES
1. Sticky feeling off-center, or poor recovery	1a. Steering wheel bind at steering column.
	1b. Steering gear shaft bind in column.
	1c. Excessive gear mesh preload.
	1d. Interference of pitman arm and valve sleeve at ball stud connection.

TROUBLESHOOTING—(Continued)

TROUBLES   CAUSES

TROUBLES	CAUSES
	1e. Interference of ball stud in "T" slot of valve sleeve.
	1f. Ball stud adjustment too tight.
	1g. Adjustment of valve spool nut too tight.
	1h. Binding valve spool.
	1i. Excessive breakaway friction of cylinder rod seal.
	1j. Steering linkage bind.
	1k. Damaged valve sleeve housing.
2. Excessive free-play or lost motion in steering	2a. Improper sector shaft or mesh preload.
	2b. Improper valve sleeve ball stud adjustment.
	2c. Improper valve adjustment.
	2d. Excessive play in steering linkage.
	2e. Excessive negative caster.
	2f. Defective valve center spring.
3. Loss of power assist	3a. Inoperative pump.
	3b. Damaged lines.
	3c. Internal parts of power cylinder broken or damaged.
	3d. Extreme maladjustment of valve spool.
4. Loss of power—one direction	4a. Maladjustment of valve spool in valve.
	4b. Inoperative by-pass check valve.
5. Oil leaks	5a. Loose or damaged hose connection.
	5b. Leaking valve seals.
	5c. Leaking cylinder seals.
6. Hard steering	6a. Low pump output.
	6b. Improper gear mesh preload.
	6c. Sticky valve.
	6d. Excessive valve leakage.
	6e. Excessive cylinder leakage.
	6f. Linkage bind.
	6g. Improper lubrication.
	6h. Improper valve spool adjustment.
	6i. Improper ball stud adjustment.
7. Chatter	7a. Loose cylinder housing.

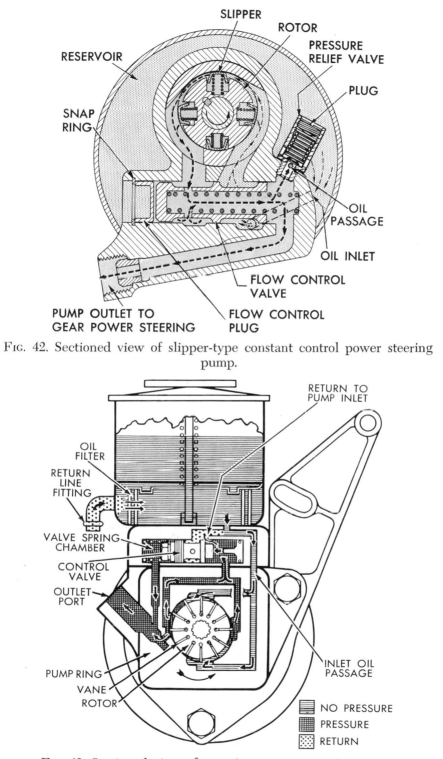

SLIPPER
ROTOR
PRESSURE
RELIEF VALVE
RESERVOIR
PLUG
SNAP
RING
OIL
PASSAGE
OIL INLET
FLOW CONTROL
VALVE
PUMP OUTLET TO   FLOW CONTROL
GEAR POWER STEERING   PLUG

FIG. 42. Sectioned view of slipper-type constant control power steering pump.

RETURN TO
PUMP INLET
OIL
FILTER
RETURN
LINE
FITTING
VALVE SPRING
CHAMBER
CONTROL
VALVE
OUTLET
PORT
INLET OIL
PASSAGE
PUMP RING
VANE
ROTOR

NO PRESSURE
PRESSURE
RETURN

FIG. 43. Sectioned view of vane-type power steering pump.
29

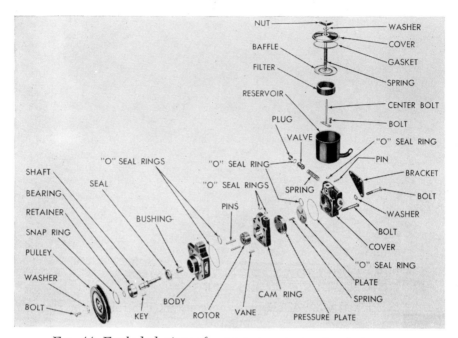

FIG. 44. Exploded view of vane-type power steering pump.

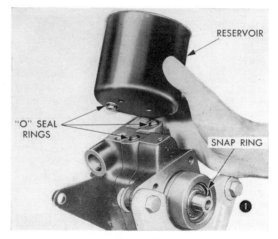

FIG. 45

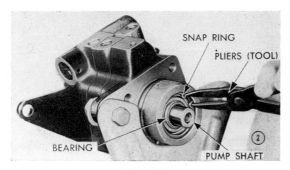

Fɪɢ. 46

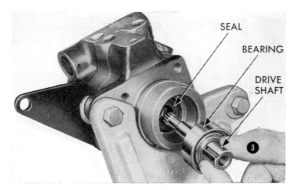

Fɪɢ. 47

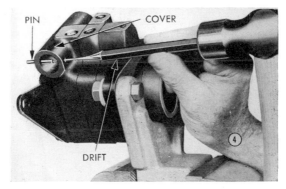

Fɪɢ. 48

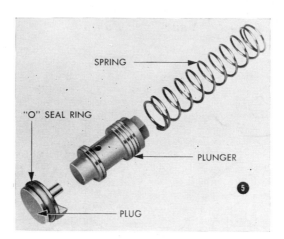

FIG. 49

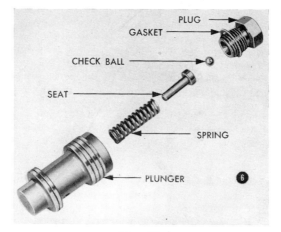

FIG. 50

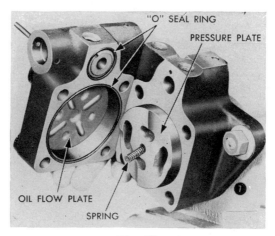

FIG. 51

32

VANE-TYPE PUMP

Disassembling:

1. Remove the pulley attaching bolt and washer, and then remove the pulley. Remove the reservoir cover, spring, baffle plate, and filter.

2. Remove the drive shaft snap ring.

3. Remove the drive shaft and bearing assembly.

4. Remove the valve retaining pin. Be careful that the valve doesn't fly out as it is under pressure.

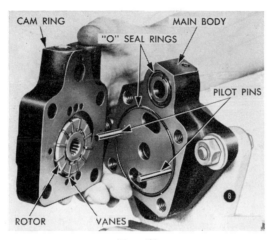

Fig. 52

5. Remove the valve plug, valve spring, and "O" ring seal.

6. Remove the hexagon plug, gasket, ball, ball seat pin, and spring.

7. Scribe an alignment mark across the bodies to assist in assembly. Then remove the screws holding the main body to the cam ring and cover. Remove the main body cover, "O" ring seal, oil flow plate, and spring. Carefully slide the pressure plate out and away from the cam ring.

8. Remove the cam ring and rotor assembly. Keep the vanes in their slots so that they will be assembled properly. Remove the dowel pins.

Cleaning and Inspecting. All parts should be cleaned in solvent and air dried with the exception of the shaft and bearing assembly. The bearing is packed with lubricant and sealed. Washing in solvent will destroy the lubricant. Order new gaskets and "O" rings.

The mating surface of the pump cover must be flat and true. The valve body should slide into the valve bore with a slight restriction

196782

and should show no signs of wear. The contact side of the pressure plate should be true and flat. It should fit tight against the rotor housing (cam ring). The sides of the rotor housing should be flat

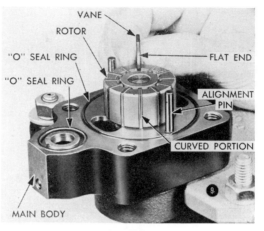

Fig. 53

and free of scratches or nicks. The oval-shaped bearing surface also should be free of scratches. The vanes should fit free in the slots with no noticeable side play. If the bushing in the main body is worn, install a new body.

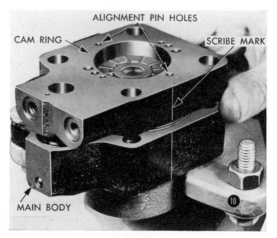

Fig. 54

Assembling. (In general, the assembly is the reverse of disassembly, therefore, only the especially important steps are illustrated.)

9. Install the bearing and shaft assembly in the main body. Secure it with the retainer snap ring (beveled side out). Install the two dowel alignment pins and the "O" ring in the contact face of the body. Install the rotor and vane assembly. Be sure that the vanes are in their original slots, with their rounded edges out.

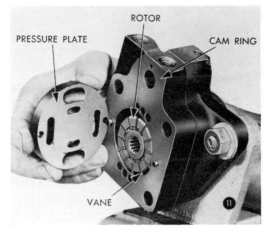

FIG. 55

10. Place the rotor housing (cam ring) over the dowels, aligning the scribe marks.

11. place the pressure plate over the dowels and against the rotor housing (cam ring) with its flat side against the cam. Center the cover over the oil flow plate and bring it up against the cam ring. Install the through bolts and tighten them to 25 to 30 foot-pounds torque.

SLEEVE-TYPE PUMP

Disassembling:

1. Remove the cap screw and reservoir.

2. Remove the inlet end cap by removing the four screws. Remove the flow spool retainer fitting. Use care because the flow valve spring is under pressure. Remove the flow spool.

3. Remove the pump body from the housing.

4. Remove the cylinder drive block and nine sleeves.

5. Remove the ball bearing retainer ring from the housing.

6. Remove the shaft and bearing assembly.

Cleaning and Inspecting. Clean all parts in solvent except the ball bearing which is sealed with lubricant. Use a lint-free rag to dry the parts.

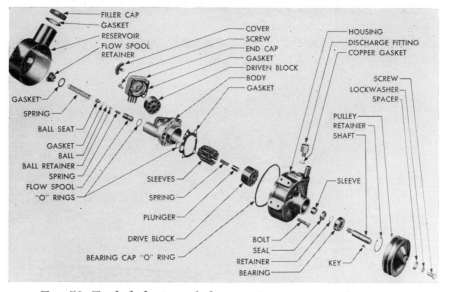

FIG. 56. Exploded view of sleeve-type power steering pump.

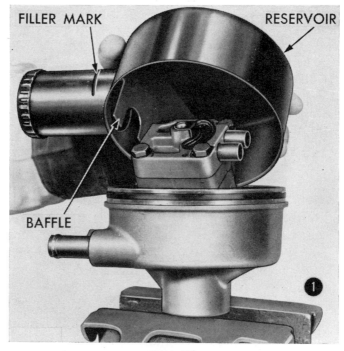

FIG. 57

Fig. 58

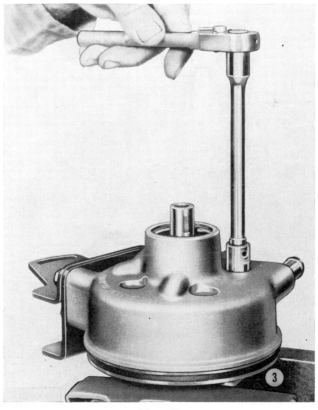

Fig. 59

37

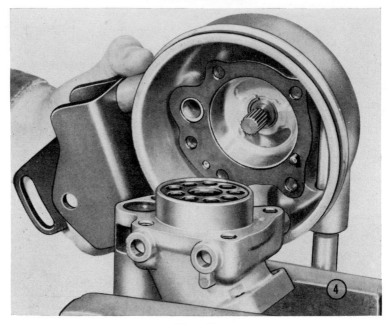

Fig. 60

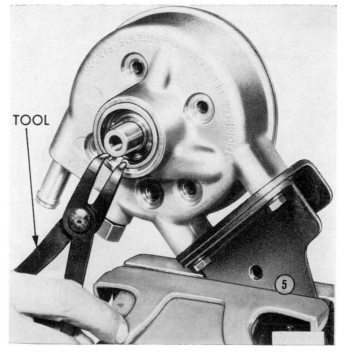

Fig. 61

FIG. 62

FIG. 63

Inspect the shaft for wear. Check the ball bearing for roughness. Examine the retaining ring groove in the housing for wear. Check the fit of the sleeves in the cylinder block bores; they must slide freely. Examine the mating surfaces of the sleeves and bores. Scored surfaces can affect pump efficiency; hairline markings are normal.

7. To check the fit of the flow spool valve, insert it in the valve body. Use a pencil to hold the inside of the valve to avoid damaging the inside diameter. Move the valve back and forth; rotate it slightly on each pass; the spool must move freely.

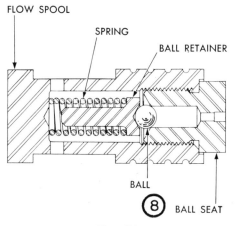

FIG. 64

8. The pressure relief valve in the flow spool valve must be able to hold the operating pressure from 750 to 900 psi. Clean the valve if it leaks.

If the operating pressure is below limits, place a $\frac{1}{32}''$ washer between the spring and ball retainer. To lower the operating pressure, place a washer between the valve seat and the flow spool body.

Assembling. (In general, the assembly is the reverse of disassembly, therefore, only the especially important steps are illustrated.)

9. Place the driven block on an assembly fixture.

10. Use SAE 10 oil to lubricate the parts. Insert the plunger spring, plunger, and seven sleeves in the drive block. Place the pump body (square end *down*) over the cylinder drive block and fixture-locating pins. Use a pointed probe to align the sleeves to a uniform spacing, and then install the other two remaining sleeves.

11. Position the serrated drive splined block over the sleeves. Sight through the bores for alignment. Lower the cylinder block

FIG. 65

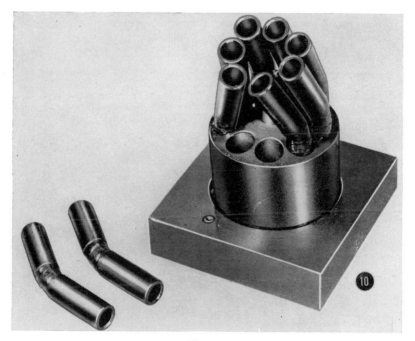

FIG. 66

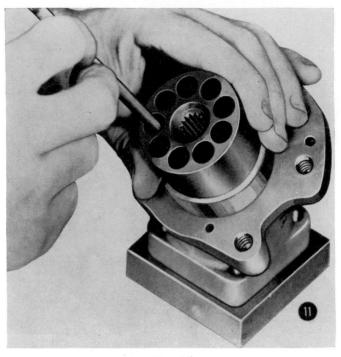

Fig. 67

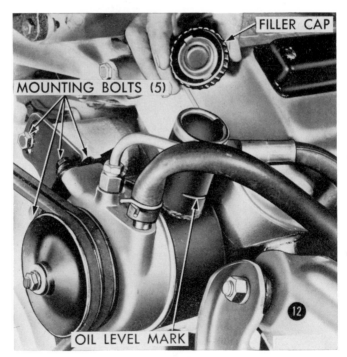

Fig. 68

until it engages the two sleeves in the forward position. Again use a probe to correct the alignment of the sleeves in the 5 and 7 o'clock positions while guiding the cylinder block downward. Continue this procedure, adjusting the position of each sleeve, until all are aligned and engaged. Push the block all the way down.

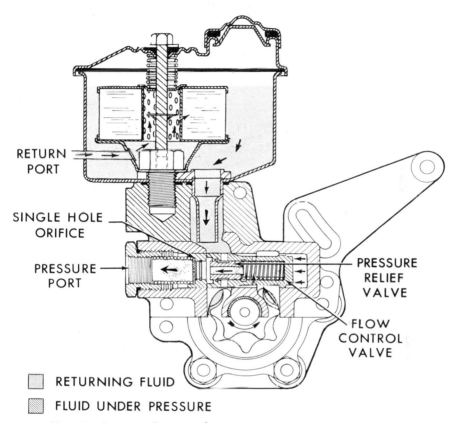

RETURN PORT

SINGLE HOLE ORIFICE

PRESSURE PORT

PRESSURE RELIEF VALVE

FLOW CONTROL VALVE

RETURNING FLUID

FLUID UNDER PRESSURE

Fɪɢ. 69. Sectioned view of rotor-type power steering pump.

12. Assemble the pump and install it on the engine. Refill the pump with Automatic Transmission Fluid Type "A" oil. Adjust the fan belt to specifications.

ACCESSORY BELT DRIVES

The satisfactory performance of belt-driven accessories depends on the maintenance of the proper belt tension. If the specified tensions are not maintained, belt slippage may cause engine overheating, lack of power assist in the steering mechanism, loss in air condi-

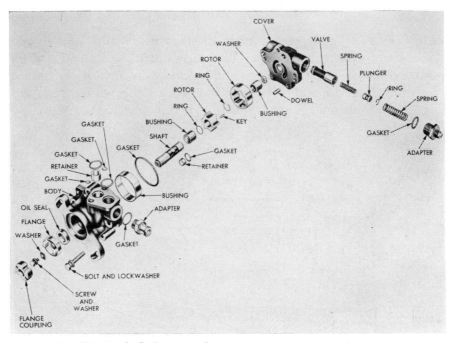

FIG. 70. Exploded view of rotor-type power steering pump.

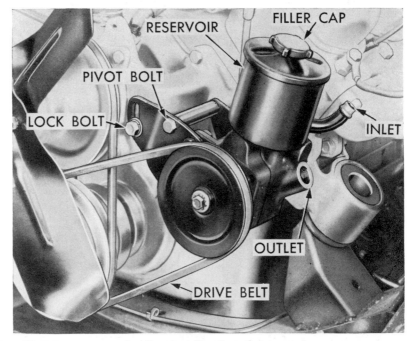

FIG. 71. Mounting and adjusting brackets of power steering pump and drive belt.

Fig. 72. Measuring belt deflection (**black arrow**) with a scale and a straightedge.

tioning capacity, reduced generator charging rates, and greatly reduced belt life.

Adjusting. There are two methods by which belts can be tensioned —the torque wrench and the deflection methods. The former is the more accurate. All belts should be adjusted to the manufacturer's specifications. Belts run over one-half hour should be adjusted to the *used* specification.

Torque Method. The torque-wrench method can be used provided that the bracket has a square hole or an adapter is available. Insert the torque wrench square drive into the square hole, loosen all the mounting bolts, and apply the specified torque to the bracket. Tighten all bolts while maintaining the torque.

Belt-Deflection Method. A belt can be adjusted by measuring the deflection of the belt at the midpoint between two pulleys under a five-pound push or pull. To make an adjustment, loosen all mounting bolts, apply tension to the bracket with a pry bar, and tighten the bolts. Recheck the deflection. It may be necessary to repeat the procedure several times until the correct deflection is obtained.

REVIEW QUESTIONS

1. From what source is the needed hydraulic pressure secured?
2. What are the two types of power steering designs in common use?
3. What is meant by a uni-directional unit?
4. What are the five types of hydraulic pumps used?
5. What is the purpose of the pressure-relief valve?
6. What type of fluid is used in each system?
7. Describe a coaxial power steering unit.
8. Describe the flow of oil with the steering valve in the neutral (center) position.
9. When the driver makes a left turn, in which direction does the spool valve move?
10. To which side of the power-assist piston is the oil directed?
11. What is the purpose of the reaction area?
12. How is driver "feel" built into the system?
13. When adjusting the unit, how is the valve body moved so that equal pressure is obtained when the gear shaft is turned slowly in each direction?
14. How does the linkage type of power steering differ from the coaxial type?
15. How is the hydraulic pressure developed?
16. What holds the control valve spool in the neutral position when the front wheels are in the straight-ahead position?
17. How much pressure is needed to overcome the pressure of the valve spool spring?
18. What happens to the valve spool when the driver releases pressure on the steering wheel?
19. In the absence of a positive operating pressure, what returns the front wheels to the straight-ahead position?
20. When making an inspection of the spool valve fit, how should it be tested?
21. When installing the unit on the car, what specified adjustment must be made?
22. When removing the valve retaining pin of the vane-type pump, what precaution is given?
23. What precaution is given about washing the shaft and bearing assembly?
24. What precaution is given in removing the flow spool retainer fitting of the sleeve-type pump?
25. What procedure is used to check the fit of the flow spool valve of the sleeve-type pump?
26. What are the two methods by which accessory belts can be tensioned?
27. Which method is the more accurate?

2

POWER BRAKES

There are two basic types of power brakes in general passenger car use. The composite unit is composed of a vacuum power unit combined with a hydraulic master cylinder; the second type contains a vacuum power unit which applies assisting pressure to a conventional brake pedal attached to a conventional master cylinder.

The Bendix and Moraine power brakes are composite units while Chrysler and Ford use the vacuum power unit combined with the conventional master cylinder.

Power brakes use engine manifold vacuum for their power. They consist of three basic elements: (1) a vacuum power cylinder, (2) a hydraulic master cylinder, and (3) a mechanically actuated control valve which regulates the degree of brake application or release in accordance with the foot pressure applied to the brake pedal.

Power brakes are designed to reduce the pedal effort required to stop the vehicle. Should failure occur in the vacuum power system, the brakes may be applied by a greater physical effort.

COMPOSITE UNIT

Principle of Operation (Bendix Treadle-Vac Hydraulic Reaction Type):

Application. As the brakes are applied by the driver, the valve operating rod moves the valve plunger to the *right* to *close* the atmospheric port. Further movement of the valve plunger *opens* the vacuum port, which allows vacuum to be applied to the right side of the power piston. With a partial vacuum on the right side of the piston, and atmospheric pressure on the left, the vacuum piston and hydraulic plunger move to the *right*. Initial movement of the hydraulic plunger allows the compensating valve to seat which closes off the return passage between the fluid reservoir and hydraulic cylinder. As pressure is developed within the hydraulic cylinder, fluid is forced through the residual check valve and brake lines to the wheel cylinders. This same pressure, acting against the rubber membrane on the end of the hydraulic plunger, transmits a

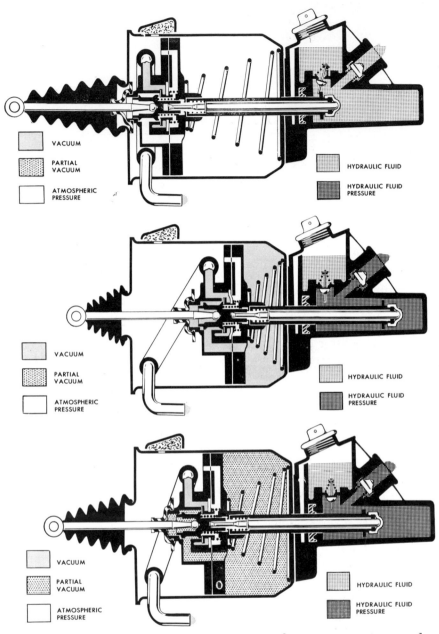

FIG. 73 (*top*). In the *released* position, atmospheric pressure is vented to both sides of diaphragm.

FIG. 74 (*center*). In the *applied* position, vacuum is admitted to rear side of diaphragm and air pressure pushes diaphragm to right.

FIG. 75 (*bottom*). In the *holding* position, both the atmospheric and the vacuum valve ports are closed, thus equalizing pressure on both sides of diaphragm.

force through the reaction rod and counter reaction spring to the *left* against the valve plunger which tends to *close* the vacuum port and bring the power piston to rest. Since the reaction force is in proportion to the hydraulic pressure developed within the hydraulic system, it gives the driver a "feel" of the amount of braking.

Holding. With pedal pressure held constant, the vacuum and atmospheric ports of the poppet valve are closed, and no further movement of the power piston occurs.

Release. When pedal pressure is removed, the valve operating rod and the valve plunger are returned to the *released* position by the valve return spring which *closes* the vacuum port and *opens* the atmospheric port. With the power piston balanced to atmospheric pressure on both sides, the power piston return spring returns the power piston and hydraulic plunger to the *released* position. When the hydraulic plunger approaches the released end of its stroke, a washer contacts the compensating valve stem to open the compensating valve port and bleed any remaining pressure back to the reservoir.

Disassembling. Each of the following steps is illustrated. The number in the lower corner of the illustration agrees with the numbered steps below.

1. Hold the Treadle-Vac in a vise and remove the rubber dust guard (1) and the felt (2) from the valve push rod. Bend out the tabs (3) on the end plate and remove the end plate (4) and the

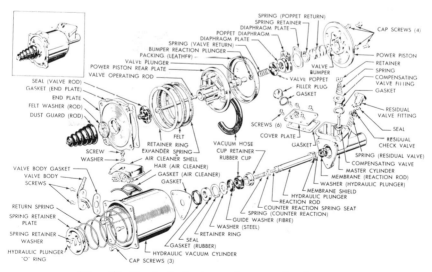

FIG. 76. Exploded view of power brake unit.

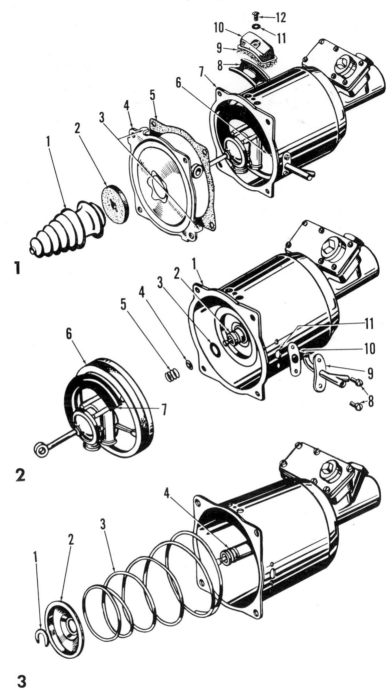

FIGS. 77, 78, AND 79

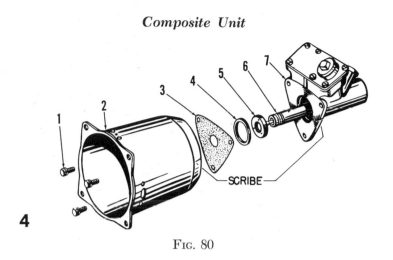

SCRIBE

F_IG. 80

gasket (5). Slide the vacuum hose (6) off the vacuum tube attached to the vacuum cylinder (7). Remove the air cleaner attaching screw (12) and separate gasket (11). Then remove the shell (10), the hair (9), and the rubber seal (8).

2. Remove the tube and plate attaching screws (8), tube and plate (9), and the gasket (10). Remove the burrs from the inside of the vacuum cylinder at the air cleaner and vacuum tube attaching screw holes. Pull out the vacuum piston and valve assembly (6) from the vacuum cylinder (1). Remove the counter reaction spring (5) and the washer (4) from the end of the hydraulic plunger (2). Then remove the "O" ring seal (3) from the groove in the hydraulic plunger.

3. Push in on the spring retainer plate (2) enough to release the C washer (1). Slide the C washer out of the groove in the hydraulic plunger (4). Remove the retainer plate (2) and the vacuum piston return spring (3).

4. Scribe across the vacuum cylinder (2) and the hydraulic master cylinder (7). Hold the hydraulic master cylinder in a vise and remove the three vacuum cylinder attaching screws and lockwashers (1). Lift off the vacuum cylinder, and remove the Vellumoid gasket (3) and the rubber ring gasket (4). Push the hydraulic plunger (6) into the hydraulic cylinder and remove the leather seal (5) from the hydraulic master cylinder flange recess.

5. Scribe across the hydraulic cylinder and cover (3). Remove the filler plug (2), and then remove the six cover attaching screws (1), the cover (3), and the gasket (4). Remove the compensating valve (5). Loosen the outlet fitting (6), but do not remove it at this time. Remove the retainer ring (7). Pull the hydraulic plunger (12) out

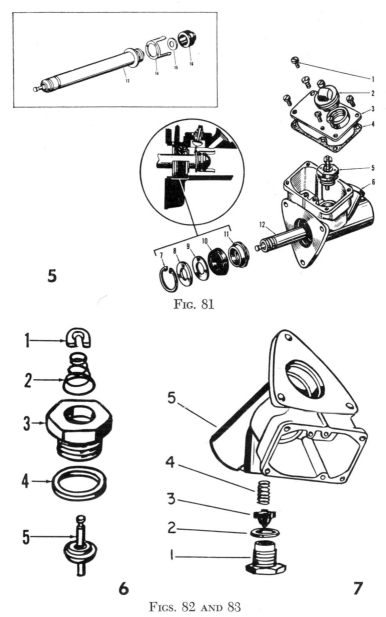

5

Fig. 81

6   7

Figs. 82 and 83

of the hydraulic cylinder and remove the steel washer (8), fiber guide washer (9), the rubber cup (10), and the cup retainer (11) from the hydraulic plunger. Remove the membrane seal (15) and the Teflon washer (14) from the hydraulic plunger (13).

6. Clamp the compensating valve fitting (3) in a vise. Spread and remove the spring retainer (1). Then remove the spring (2), the valve stem and poppet (5), and the fitting gasket (4) from the compensating valve fitting.

7. Remove the hydraulic cylinder from the vise, and then remove the outlet fitting (1), the residual check valve spring (4), the valve cup and retainer (3) from the hydraulic cylinder (5). Remove the gasket (2) from the fitting (1).

8. Remove the valve rod seal and stop (23) from the piston (27)

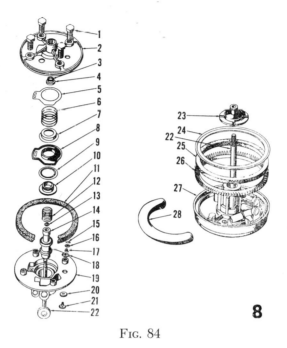

FIG. 84

and the valve operating rod (22). Remove the vacuum hose (28) from the tube on the rear piston plate. Remove the felt retainer ring (24), the felt (25), and the expander spring (26) from the rear piston plate. Turn the piston over, clamp the rear piston plate (19) in a vise, and remove the four cap screws (1), the front piston plate (2), the diaphragm plate (5), and the return spring (6). Drive out the fiber washer (4) and remove the rubber bumper (3) from the front piston plate (2). Remove the diaphragm parts group (7 through 10) as an assembly, and then separate the parts. Lift off the leather piston packing (11) and return spring (12). Remove the valve plunger (14) with the valve operating rod (22) from the rear piston plate and remove the rubber bumper (13) from the end of the valve plunger (14).

On units where the diameter of the valve operating rod end is larger than the hole in the piston, hold the assembly with the valve plunger (14) down and inject alcohol in the valve plunger opening around the rod to wet the rubber lock. Then drive the valve plunger off the valve operating rod.

On units with the pressure relief valve in the rear piston plate, do not remove the relief valve except when necessary. To remove it, hold your finger against the end of the valve poppet (21) and remove the hair pin lock (15), spring retainer washer (16), spring (17), and the poppet guide washer (18). Then remove the valve from the piston plate. Remove the rubber seal (20) from the valve stem and washer.

Cleaning and Inspecting. Clean all parts in solvent and dry with compressed air. After cleaning, parts which come into contact with hydraulic brake fluid must be rewashed in clean alcohol.

Replace all worn or damaged parts. All rubber parts must be replaced.

Assembling:

1. Before assembling any rubber part, it must be dipped in brake fluid. Insert the grooved end of the compensating valve poppet and stem (5) through the hole in the fitting (3) from the threaded end. Assemble the large diameter end of the spring (2) over the stem,

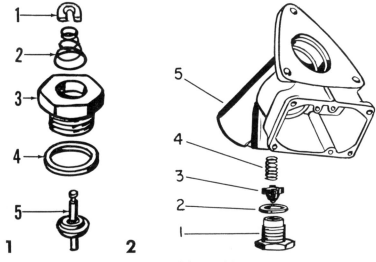

FIGS. 85 AND 86

hold the valve poppet on its seat, compress the spring, and assemble the retainer washer (1) in the groove of the valve stem. Squeeze the ends of the washer together with pliers. Assemble a new gasket (4) over the threads of the compensating valve fitting.

2. Assemble a new gasket (2) over the threads of the hydraulic outlet fitting (1). Hold the outlet fitting in a vertical position and insert the cone end of the cup and retainer (3) in the fitting. Place the check valve spring (4) in the recess of the retainer. Hold the hydraulic cylinder upside down as shown, and thread the outlet fitting (1) into the hydraulic cylinder finger-tight.

3. Hold the hydraulic cylinder in a vise. Apply a light coating of Silicone grease D-4 or D-5 to the Telfon washer (14) and to the rubber membrane (15), and assemble the washer and membrane to the end of the hydraulic plunger (13). Insert the membrane end of the plunger (12) in the cylinder and assemble the seal parts over the end of the plunger as follows: cup retainer (11) (with its counterbored side away from the washer on the plunger), cup (10), fiber guide washer (9), and the steel spacer washer (8). Slide the seal parts into the recess of the cylinder, push the plunger in to the end of its stroke, and assemble the retainer ring (7) in the ring groove. Assemble the compensating valve (5) in the threaded hole of the cylinder and securely tighten it. Place a new cover gasket (4) on the hydraulic cylinder, align the cover to the scribe marks, replace, and securely tighten the cover screws (1). Place a new gasket on the filler cap (2) and assemble the filler cap. Securely tighten the outlet fitting (6).

4. Pull out the hydraulic plunger (6), place a seal assembly tool (8) over the end of the plunger, and assemble the leather seal (5) over the seal tool (lip of leather toward the hydraulic cylinder). Press the seal into the recess of the hydraulic cylinder, and then remove the tool. Place a gasket (4) in the recess of the hydraulic cylinder. Insert three cap screws (1) through holes in the end of the vacuum cylinder (2) and the holes in the gasket (3). Align the vacuum cylinder and the hydraulic cylinder to the scribe marks. Assemble three cap screws and tighten them securely. Wipe out the inside of the vacuum cylinder, and then pull out the hydraulic plunger to the end of its stroke.

5. Place the larger diameter end of the vacuum piston return spring (3) in the vacuum cylinder, and assemble the retainer plate (2) over the end of the hydraulic plunger (4). Compress the spring

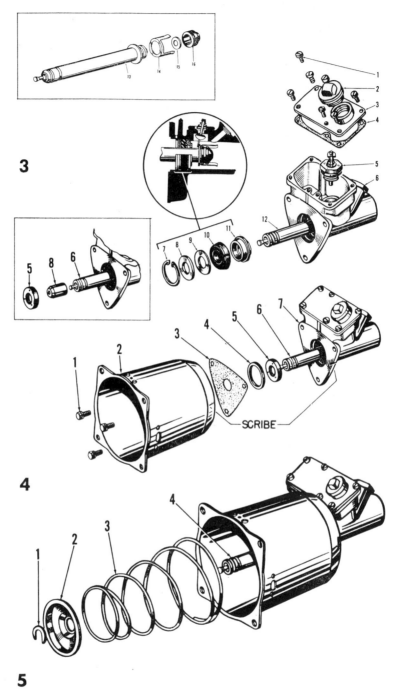

SCRIBE

Figs. 87, 88, and 89

and assemble the C washer in the second groove of the hydraulic plunger.

6. If the valve operating rod (22) and the valve plunger (14) are separated, assemble the valve operating rod to the valve plunger as follows: dip the valve plunger in alcohol before inserting the valve rod (make sure that the ball end of the rod is locked in place in the valve plunger; It may be necessary to tap the end of the valve

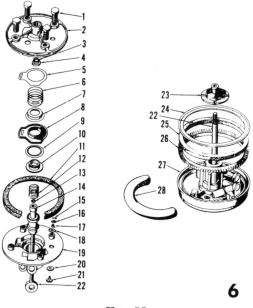

Fig. 90

operating rod to seat the ball end in the valve plunger), insert the valve operating rod through the hole in the rear piston plate, assemble the bumper (13) in the end of the valve plunger, and assemble the spring (12) over the end of the plunger.

On units where the eye end of the rod is larger than the hole in the rear piston plate, it will be necessary to insert the end of the valve operating rod through the piston plate before assembling the valve operating rod and valve plunger.

On units with the pressure relief valve removed, assemble the relief valve as follows: place the poppet guide washer (18) in the recess of the rear piston plate, dip the valve seal (20) in alcohol, and assemble the seal over the valve stem and washer (21). Insert the valve stem through the hole in the piston plate and guide washer.

Then assemble the spring (17), the washer (16), and the hair pin retainer (15).

Assemble the leather packing (11) on the piston with the lip side toward the valve operating rod. Assemble the round diaphragm plate (9) in the groove of the diaphragm (8), and then assemble the diaphragm over the shoulder of the valve poppet (10). Place this assembly in the recess of the piston plate and assemble the spring retainer (7) and the diaphragm plate (5) in the relief of the diaphragm. Assemble the poppet return spring (6) over the flange of the spring retainer.

Remove the burrs from the center bore of the front piston plate (2) and assemble the rubber bumper (3) and the fiber washer (4) in the recess of the plate from the side as shown. Stake the fiber washer in place at three points. Place the front piston plate on the rear piston plate (make certain that the by-pass holes are in alignment) and assemble four attaching cap screws (1) finger-tight.

Place the assembly ring over the piston leather. Turn the piston assembly upside down, and assemble the expander spring (26) against the inside lip of the leather packing. Dip the felt in vacuum cylinder oil and assemble it against the expander spring. Assemble the retainer plate (24) making certain that the plate is securely anchored in the grooves at four projections of the piston assembly. Securely tighten the screws. Dip the valve rod seal and bumper (23) in brake fluid, and assemble it over the end of the valve operating rod (22) making certain that the rod is seated in the groove of the piston assembly.

7. Apply a thin film of vacuum cylinder oil to the inside of the cylinder (1). Assemble the "O" ring seal (3) in the outer groove of the hydraulic plunger (2). Then assemble the washer (4) and the counter reaction spring (5) in the counter bore of the plunger. Assemble the hose (7) on the tube of the piston. Insert the piston in the cylinder with the free end of the hose in line with the center of the elongated hole (11) for the vacuum tube. Place a new gasket (10) on the tube and plate (9). Slide the hose on the tube about ⅝", and attach the tube and plate with the screws (8). Operate the piston through its full stroke several times to make certain that the hose does not rub against the cylinder or piston. Reposition the hose if necessary.

8. On units with an integral air cleaner, assemble the rubber seal (8) on the edges of the air cleaner shell (10). Attach the air cleaner to the vacuum cylinder using a new screw (12) and gasket (11). With a six inch scale, push the hair (9) into the open spaces at each end of the air cleaner. Align the holes on the end plate (4) and

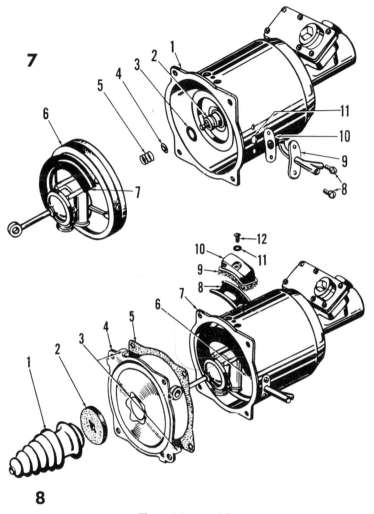

FIGS. 91 AND 92

gasket (5) with the holes in the flange of the cylinder. Bend over the two tabs on the end plate to lock it. Assemble the valve rod felt (2) in either the first or second fold of the rubber guard (1). Dip the small end of the guard in brake fluid and assemble the guard and felt over the flange at the center of the end plate.

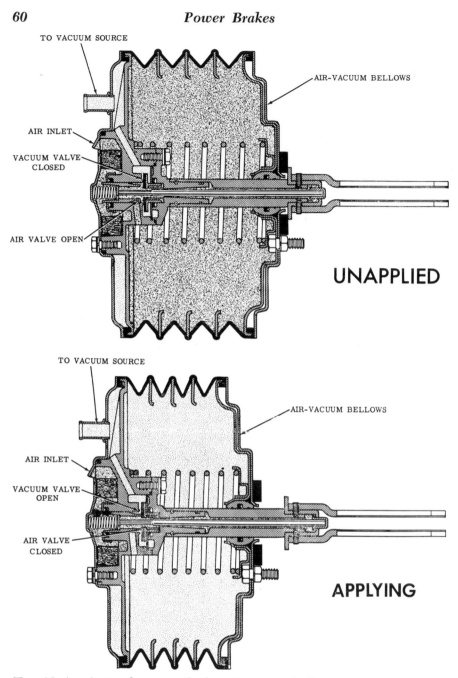

TO VACUUM SOURCE

AIR-VACUUM BELLOWS

AIR INLET

VACUUM VALVE
CLOSED

AIR VALVE OPEN

UNAPPLIED

TO VACUUM SOURCE

AIR-VACUUM BELLOWS

AIR INLET

VACUUM VALVE
OPEN

AIR VALVE
CLOSED

APPLYING

FIG. 93 (*top*). In the *unapplied* position, air bellows-type booster unit maintains an *open* air inlet valve and a *closed* vacuum valve; thus no pressure is developed in the unit.

FIG. 94 (*bottom*). In the *applying* position, vacuum valve is *opened* and air valve is *closed*.

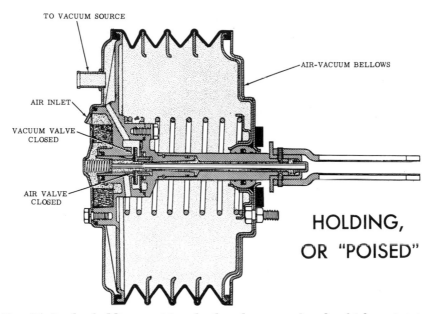

TO VACUUM SOURCE

AIR-VACUUM BELLOWS

AIR INLET

VACUUM VALVE
CLOSED

AIR VALVE
CLOSED

HOLDING,
OR "POISED"

Fɪɢ. 95. In the *holding* position, both valves are closed, which maintains equal pressure on both sides of piston.

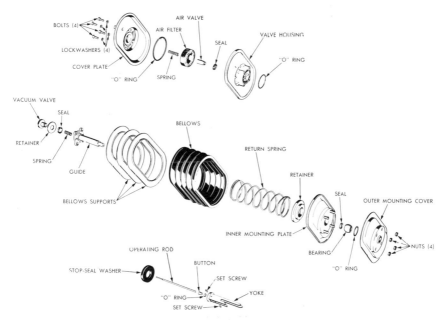

BOLTS (4)

AIR VALVE

AIR FILTER

VALVE HOUSING

LOCKWASHERS (4)

SEAL

"O" RING

COVER PLATE

"O" RING

SPRING

VACUUM VALVE

SEAL

BELLOWS

RETURN SPRING

RETAINER

SEAL

OUTER MOUNTING COVER

RETAINER

SPRING

GUIDE

BELLOWS SUPPORTS

INNER MOUNTING PLATE

BEARING

NUTS (4)

"O" RING

OPERATING ROD

STOP-SEAL WASHER

BUTTON

SET SCREW

"O" RING

YOKE

SET SCREW

Fɪɢ. 96. Exploded view of bellows-type power brake unit.

Fig. 97

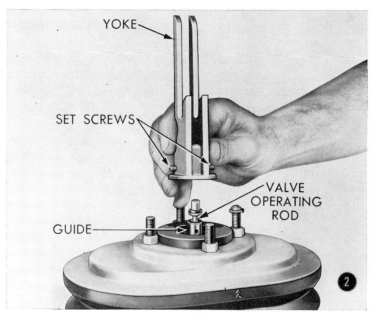

YOKE

SET SCREWS

VALVE
OPERATING
ROD

GUIDE

Fig. 98

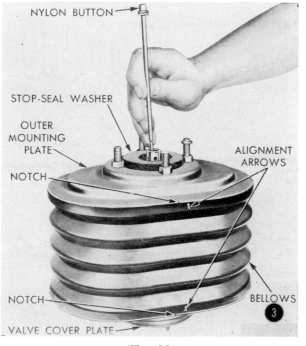

NYLON BUTTON

STOP-SEAL WASHER

OUTER
MOUNTING
PLATE

NOTCH

ALIGNMENT
ARROWS

NOTCH

BELLOWS

VALVE COVER PLATE

Fig. 99

POWER BRAKE UNIT (BELLOWS TYPE)

The bellows-type booster unit is a vacuum bellows connected mechanically to the brake pedal. Power is applied only when the unit is assisting with a brake application, otherwise, no linkage connection exists. With a loss of engine vacuum, the brake pedal is free to move independently of the power booster unit.

Disassembling. Each of the following steps is illustrated. The number in the lower right hand corner of the illustration agrees with the numbered steps below.

1. Remove the nuts that attach the mounting plate to the unit. Slide the plate off and away. Remove and discard the mounting plate "O" ring.

2. Slightly compress the bellows by hand and use an Allen wrench to loosen the two setscrews enough to remove the yoke. Slide the yoke off the end of the guide and away from the unit.

3. Remove the rubber stop seal washer. Lift the valve operating rod out of the unit. Remove and discard the valve operating rod button seal.

4. Remove the nuts that attach the outer mounting plate. Use a

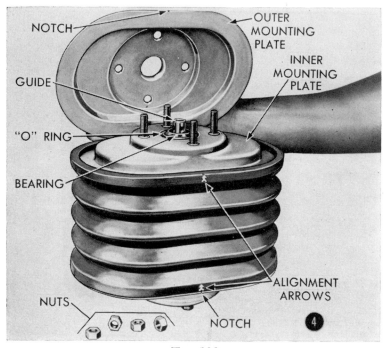

Fig. 100

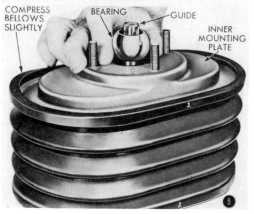

Fig. 101

screwdriver to pry up gently. Lift the plate straight up and away from the unit. Discard the "O" ring.

5. Compress the bellows by hand enough to expose the guide bearing. Slide the bearing off the end of the guide. Remove and discard the bearing seal from inside of the bearing.

6. Peel back the outer lip of the bellows around the inner mount-

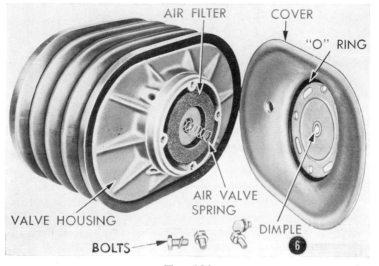

FIG. 102

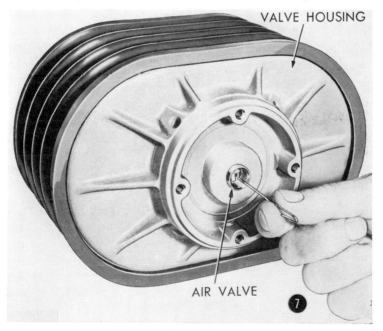

FIG. 103

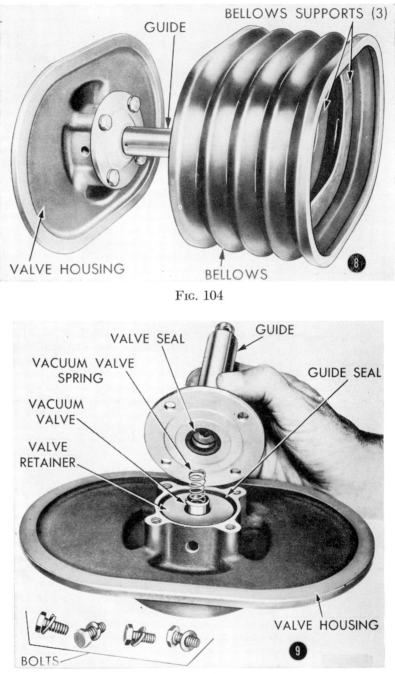

GUIDE

BELLOWS SUPPORTS (3)

VALVE HOUSING

BELLOWS

Fig. 104

VALVE SEAL

GUIDE

VACUUM VALVE
SPRING

GUIDE SEAL

VACUUM
VALVE

VALVE
RETAINER

VALVE HOUSING

BOLTS

Fig. 105

ing plate. Keep one hand on the plate to prevent it from snapping up. Remove the plate and lift out the return spring and the return spring retainer. Place the unit on its side and remove the bolts and lockwashers that attach the valve cover to the valve. Lift off the cover. Extreme care should be taken to avoid scratching the inner face of the plate where it clamps to the bellows flange, otherwise, it will leak. Remove the "O" ring from the valve cover and discard it. Remove the air valve spring from the center of the valve.

7. Remove the air filter and slide the air valve out of the housing. To remove the valve, it may be necessary to use a hook formed from a paper clip.

8. Place the valve housing, end down, on the bench. Remove the bellows from the valve by peeling back the outer lip of the bellows. Lift the bellows up and away from the valve. If a new bellows is to be installed, remove the three bellows supports.

9. Remove the bolts and lockwashers that attach the guide to the valve body. Lift off the guide to expose the vacuum valve, valve spring, and seals. Remove and discard the seals.

10. Lift out the vacuum valve and the retainer. Remove and discard the valve housing-to-guide seal. Invert the valve housing and remove the air valve seal from its groove in the valve body.

Cleaning and Inspecting. Clean all parts, except the bellows, bearing, and air filter in solvent, and blow the parts dry with compressed air. If necessary, the bellows may be washed with water and mild soap.

Inspect all parts for wear or damage. Inspect the check air valve for signs of scoring or wear. If the valve body or the valve is scored or worn, install new parts. Always use new "O" rings and new seal rings.

Assembling. (In general, the assembly is the reverse of disassembly, therefore, only the most important steps are illustrated.)

11. Lubricate all seals and "O" rings with silicone grease. Insert the new air valve seal into the bore of the valve housing. The lips of the seal should face out. Carefully position a new vacuum valve in the retainer. Invert the valve housing and install the vacuum valve and retainer in the housing. Press down firmly on the retainer to snap it in place. Position a new valve housing-to-guide seal in the groove provided.

12. Install a new vacuum valve seal in the bore guide. The lip of the seal should be positioned toward the bottom of the bore. Install the vacuum valve spring in the center of the valve. Position the guide over the vacuum valve, lining up the bolt in the guide with the bolt holes in the valve body. Carefully lower the guide down against the valve body, making certain that the tapered portion of the vacuum valve enters the seal evenly. Press down on the guide to seat it and install the bolts and lockwashers. Tighten the bolts evenly and securely. Be sure that the countersunk holes at the end of the guide line up with the long centerline of the valve housing.

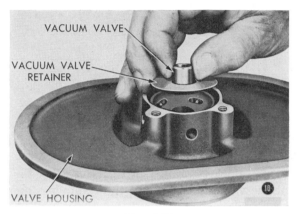

Fig. 106

13. If new bellows are being installed, position the supports in the bellows. They must be centered in three center accordion folds and aligned with the bellows and with each other. Using a holding fixture to support the guide and valve assembly, install the bellows. Be sure that the arrows on the edge of the bellows and the housing are aligned.

14. With the assembly in a holding fixture, lightly coat the outer surface of the air valve with silicone grease, and insert it into the bore of the housing (small end first). Use finger pressure to test for free movement of the valve against the vacuum valve spring.

15. Install the air valve spring in the recess of the air valve, and then install the air filter. Install a new valve housing cover "O" ring on the shoulder provided on the valve body hub. Position the valve body cover over the valve housing, with the notch in the edge of the cover matching the arrow on the bellows. Be sure that the air valve spring nestles on the dimple in the center of the cover. Press the cover down evenly over the valve housing to seat the cover "O" ring. Install the bolts and tighten them securely.

16. Remove the assembly from the holding fixture and invert the

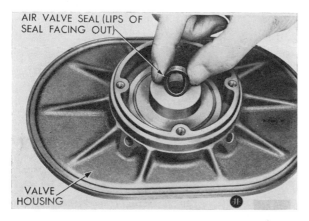

AIR VALVE SEAL (LIPS OF SEAL FACING OUT)

VALVE HOUSING

FIG. 107

FIG. 108

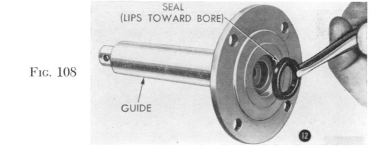

SEAL (LIPS TOWARD BORE)

GUIDE

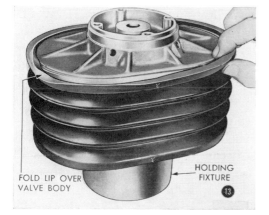

FOLD LIP OVER VALVE BODY

HOLDING FIXTURE

FIG. 109

unit. Lightly coat the guide with silicone grease and install the return spring. Position the spring evenly around the hub of the valve housing and guide. Place the spring retainer and the inner mounting plate over the spring, being sure the arrow, stamped on the plate, is in line with the arrow on the edge of the bellows.

17. Compress the return spring and fold the bellows lip over the edge of the plate. Be sure that the bellows fit evenly all around the

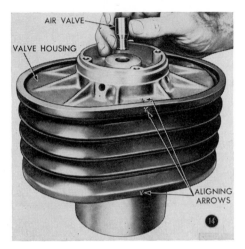

Fig. 110

plate. Install a new guide bearing seal in the groove inside of the bearing bore. The seal must nest snugly in the bearing. Using silicone grease, lubricate the inside of the bearing, and slide it over the guide while compressing the bellows. The bearing must be installed with the lip of the seal facing out. Push the bearing down over the guide and into the pocket of the plate. Release the bellows and the bearing will ride up the guide with the plate and into position.

Install the bearing-to-mounting plate "O" ring, and lower the outer mounting plate down on the assembly. The notch on the edge of the plate must be in line with the arrow on the bellows. Install the nuts and draw them down finger-tight. Slide a new valve operating rod seal ring over the nylon bumper on the end of the rod and press it into the groove. Install the rod in the center of the guide. Press on the end of the rod to test for free operation or movement of the air and vacuum valves. A "two-step" movement should be felt when the rod is depressed and released fully. Place a new stop seal washer in position, and install the yoke on the end of the guide. Compress the bellows slightly, and alternately tighten the setscrews.

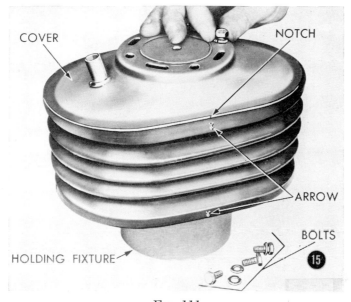

Fig. 111

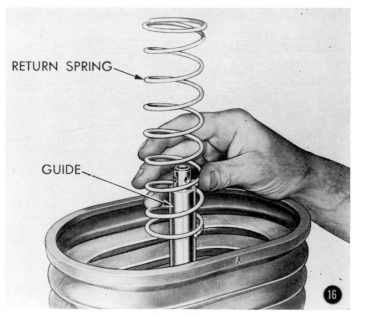

Fig. 112

The hub of the yoke must be down snug against the shoulder of the guide with the setscrews aligned with the tapered hole in the guide. Tighten the mounting plate nuts securely.

18. Place the mounting bracket in position, with the long centerline of the bracket at right angles to the long centerline of the unit

INNER MOUNTING COVER

BEARING

TAPERED HOLES (SET SCREW)

GUIDE

Fig. 113

section. Install the nuts and lockwashers, and tighten them securely. Position the assembled unit on the dash panel so that its axis inclines down toward the front of the car. As the yoke passes through the dash panel, be sure that the unit engages the pedal linkage correctly. The yoke must slide over the nylon bushings on the power brake lever cross pin. Install and connect the master cylinder. Replace the four hex nuts and lockwashers. Tighten them securely.

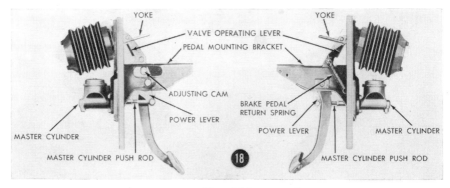

YOKE   YOKE

VALVE OPERATING LEVER
PEDAL MOUNTING BRACKET

ADJUSTING CAM
BRAKE PEDAL
RETURN SPRING
POWER LEVER
POWER LEVER

MASTER CYLINDER   MASTER CYLINDER

MASTER CYLINDER PUSH ROD   MASTER CYLINDER PUSH ROD

Fig. 114

19. After installation, a "free-play" adjustment must be made at *no vacuum*. (Removing the vacuum hose and pressing the brake pedal several times will aid in obtaining a no-vacuum condition.)

To make this test, insert the blade of a screwdriver between the rubber collar of the power brake trigger pivot and the rear side of the elongated hole in the power brake lever to force them apart. Free pedal play should be between $\frac{1}{32}''$ and $\frac{1}{8}''$. An adjustment can be made by lengthening or shortening the master cylinder push rod.

It should seldom be necessary to adjust the brake pedal trigger arm. However, such an adjustment may be necessary to eliminate the following conditions: If the pedal pressure releases slowly, adjust by rotating the adjustment screw in a counterclockwise direction. A time delay (noted on a fast brake application) can be corrected by making a clockwise adjustment of the screw. Should the pedal vibrate (booster chatter), turn the adjusting screw counterclockwise. A more likely cause is an empty master cylinder.

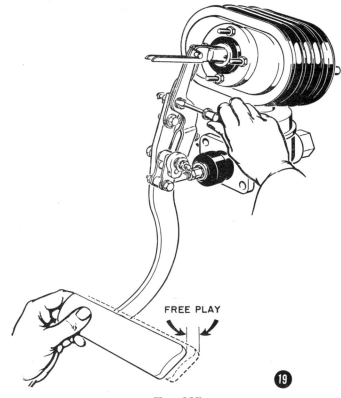

FREE PLAY

Fig. 115

TROUBLESHOOTING

TROUBLES	CAUSES
1. Hard pedal	1a. Frozen brake mechanism.
	1b. Glazed linings.
	1c. Vacuum leaks.
	1d. Collapsed hoses.
	1e. Restricted air cleaner.
	1f. Internal vacuum leaks.
2. Grabby brakes	2a. Grease on brake linings.
	2b. Brake fluid on linings.
	2c. Anchor pins out of adjustment.
	2d. Scored drums.
	2e. Malfunction in control valve portion of the piston or at the reaction rod.
3. Pedal goes to floorboard	3a. Shoes out of adjustment.
	3b. Hydraulic leaks.
	3c. Hydraulic fluid low.
	3d. Air in lines.
	3e. Internal hydraulic leak at plunger cup, reaction rod membrane, or compensating valve.
4. Brakes fail to release	4a. Frozen pedal mechanism.
	4b. Brake adjustment too tight.
	4c. Improper adjustment of anchor pins.
	4d. Excessive friction of vacuum piston.
	4e. Malfunction at fluid compensating port in the valve portion of the piston.

REVIEW QUESTIONS

1. What are the two basic types of power brakes in common use?
2. From what source is the power, which actuates the unit, obtained?
3. Of what three basic elements does a power brake unit consist?
4. What is the operating result, should failure occur in the power system?
5. What holds the power unit piston in the *released* position when no pedal pressure is being applied?
6. As the brake pedal is depressed, what happens to the atmospheric port?
7. What closes the compensating valve port?
8. What opens the compensating valve port on release of the pressure applied to the brake pedal?

9. When cleaning parts of the power brake unit, how must rubber parts be handled?
10. What must be done to rubber parts before being assembled?
11. What procedure is recommended to ensure that the hose does not rub against the cylinder or piston after it has been assembled?
12. How does the bellows-type booster unit differ from the composite-type power brake unit?
13. What happens if there is a loss of vacuum with the bellows-type brake?
14. Why should you take extreme care to avoid scratching the inner face of the bellows flange?
15. What washing procedure is suggested for the bellows?
16. What type of lubricating grease is suggested for assembling the bellows-type power unit?
17. After installing the unit on the car, what "free-play" adjustment precaution is given?
18. When is it necessary to adjust the brake pedal trigger arm?

3

AIR SUSPENSION SYSTEM

Recently, a system of four air bellows has come to replace the conventional automobile steel springs as optional equipment on many cars; such cars ride on compressed air. The air suspension system contains leveling features to overcome unequal loading and body tilt on curves.

Chrysler products use two air bellows to replace the rear springs while retaining their original torsion rod suspension in the front.

OPERATION

The engine drives a compressor which supplies air at approximately 280 psi pressure to an air storage tank. The tank acts as a reservoir and supplies air as needed to a manual override valve which reduces and regulates this 280 psi to a constant lower pressure. This is the air pressure which then is passed to three height control valves; one at each rear air spring and another that controls both front air springs. From the height control valves, air goes directly to the air springs.

Air in the springs will exhaust with removal of load and for this purpose separate return lines are provided to return air from the air springs, through the height control valves, back to the manual override valve and to a tee fitting at the compressor where the air may either be used by the compressor or may exhaust out of the air cleaner.

All of the described operation is done automatically, the same as any conventional coil sprung car. However, a control is located at the dash which must be manually operated to raise the car when the need for changing a tire and wheel arises. This feature locks out the automatic control of the height control valves.

PARTS

Compressor. A two-cylinder die-cast aluminum compressor is used. It has a maximum build-up pressure of approximately 280 psi. A single belt drives the compressor at a speed ratio of 1.15 to 1. A

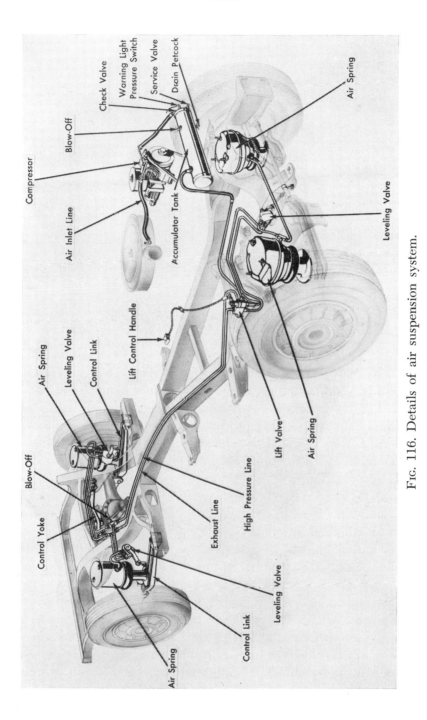

Fig. 116. Details of air suspension system.

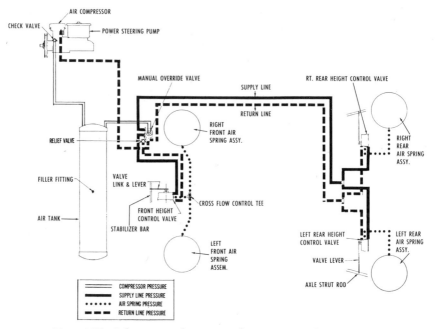

FIG. 117. Schematic diagram of air suspension system.

check valve at the air outlet fitting prevents leakage of air from the air tank through the compressor when the engine is not running.

Steel cylinder sleeves are cast in and cannot be replaced. At the top of the block are two holes for each cylinder; one air inlet and a smaller exhaust which lead to exterior holes tapped for fittings.

Air Tank. A cylindrical air tank, having a capacity of 820 cubic inches is pressurized at 280 psi and serves as an air reservoir and water trap. There are two fittings welded to the top of the tank. The one on the left is for air under pressure coming from the compressor; the other is a Schrader type valve, normally used for manually filling the tank and diagnosis. Midway on the right end, another fitting serves as the outlet. At the bottom of the left end is a valve which should be opened periodically (every 1000 miles) for draining of any water and oil which may have come through the compressor.

Air Springs. Air springs are located in the same positions as are coil springs on other models. They are air chambers consisting of metal containers, called domes, into which rubber diaphragms are positioned at the bottom. The diaphragms are compressed by means of specially shaped plungers which are below the diaphragms and connected to the suspension.

The normal pressure within the air springs is approximately 100 psi. As car weight load is increased, the height control valves allow more air to enter the springs so that the trim height remains constant. Pressure within the springs then goes up. The reverse takes place when decreasing load weight.

Manual Override Valve. The manual override valve assembly is bolted to the frame front spring cross member at the right side. One of its functions is to serve as a junction block for most of the air lines. It also reduces and regulates the high pressure coming from the tank to a static supply pressure of approximately 140 psi. Incorporated in the exhaust side of the valve is the return flow control orifice which restricts flow of air from the return lines to the atmosphere.

An important function of the override valve is to allow raising the car to its full rebound position when the need for changing a wheel or tire arises. This is done by raising a lever on the valve through a Bowden control wire which extends into the driver compartment dash.

When the lever is in its normal *down* position, the air routing is from the override valve, through air supply lines to the two height control valves in the rear and the one height control valve in front. The pressure within these lines is maintained at approximately 140

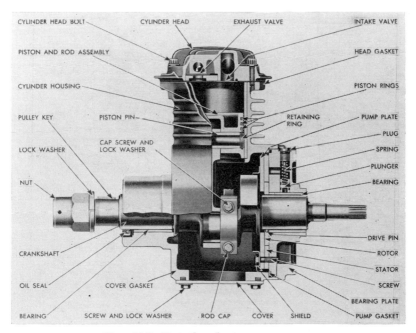

FIG. 118. Details of air compressor.

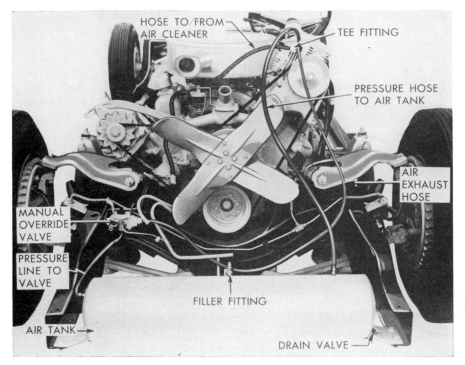

FIG. 119. Air storage tank is located across front of chassis.

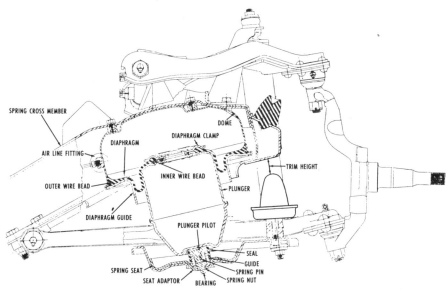

FIG. 120. Details of air spring.

psi. When the lever on the override valve is raised, the exhaust line leading to the air cleaner is shut off, and the air return lines are opened to the same pressure as in the pressure lines. This pressure feeds to the height control valves and the valves allow the car to be raised approximately 5½ inches. When the lever is returned to its normal position, the air return lines are shut off from the supply pressure and the exhaust passage leading to the return flow control orifice is opened, allowing the excess air to bleed slowly out from the return lines through this orifice until pressure lowers to atmospheric pressure.

When it becomes necessary to change a tire or wheel, or if the car must be jacked up or raised on a free-wheel hoist for any reason, the override valve must be actuated so that the car will be raised to a full rebound position. The car may then be raised in the conventional manner.

Height Control Valves. Three height control valves are used; one for each rear wheel and one for both front wheels. All the valves are identical in construction and operation with the exception of the lever arms which are longer on the rear valves. The valves work together to keep the trim height of the car constant regardless of weight load or level of the ground. They do this by controlling the air flow into or out of the air springs.

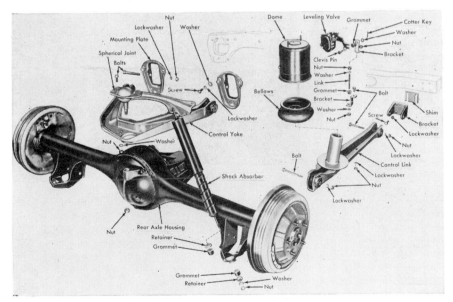

Fig. 121. Disassembled view of rear air spring.

Fig. 122. Location of manual override valve.

Each rear height control valve is mounted to a bracket by two cap screws. The two holes in the bracket are elongated to allow positioning of the valves when trim height corrections are necessary. The valve operating arms are connected to links which in turn are bolted to the rear axle strut rods. Vertical motion of either rear wheel will move the link and therefore the arm. The direction of vertical motion will determine whether the valves will allow the air springs to take in more air or exhaust some of the existing air.

The front height control valve is located on a bracket inside of the front spring cross member and in line with the center line of the car. One end of a link is connected to the valve arm with the other end connected to a lever. The lever is clamped to the stabilizer bar and allows for positioning of the front height control valve when trim height corrections are needed at the front. Whenever either front wheel or both move up or down, the stabilizer bar will twist and transfer this motion to the valve link and arm. The valve will then allow the air spring to either exhaust or take in additional air, depending on the direction the wheel moves.

To prevent the valves from opening and closing each time a small bump is struck, a "dwell" period is built into the mechanism. The wheels can raise or lower about ⅜″ above or below the "normal" trim line before the valves are actuated.

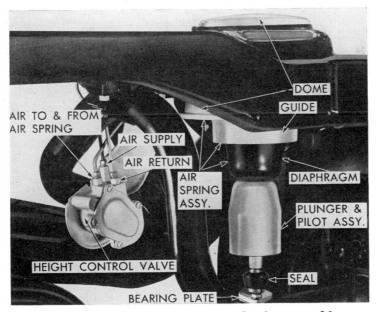

Fig. 123. Details of rear spring and valve assembly.

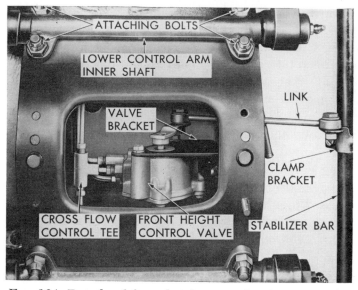

Fig. 124. Details of front height control valve assembly.

To reduce sensitivity, an orifice is built into all intake and exhaust valve fittings. Since the compression-rebound cycle of the air spring is of such short duration, these restrictions allow very little air movement during the short time the valves are open.

When a car is at curb weight, the trim height will be correct. As soon as weight is added, such as the addition of passengers, the car lowers and the height control valve arm moves up. A Schrader-type valve in the air supply (intake) fitting is mechanically opened. A second Schrader valve in the fitting is opened by supply-line pressure. With both intake valves open and the exhaust closed, air is allowed to flow into the air springs, until the car is raised to its normal trim height and all valves are closed.

When weight is removed and the car raises, the valve arms move down and open the Schrader-type exhaust valves, thereby allowing excess air to pass out of the air springs until the car lowers to its normal trim height and the valves close.

Cross Flow Control Tee. To improve cornering stability, a crossflow tee is provided for the front air springs. It is inserted in the air supply line between the air springs and the height control valve and attached to the height control valve. Inside the tee are two check balls, one for each spring, which are forced off their seats when the air flows toward the air springs, but are forced against the seats when air flows from the springs. The seats, however, have metered orifices which allow a restricted flow of air. Therefore, when cornering, air from the high pressured spring cannot flow freely to the spring with lesser pressure.

Return Flow Control Orifice. The return flow control orifice is located in the manual override valve on the exhaust side. As air exhausts from the air springs under certain conditions, such as when unloading the car, it flows through the exhaust, or return lines, to the override valve and through the return flow control orifice. This orifice allows only a gradual flow from the return lines to the atmosphere. Once through the orifice, the air flows to a tee fitting and then to either the compressor or the air cleaner.

Thus, some back pressure is retained in the exhaust lines to give additional control when rounding curves, during braking or when accelerating.

For instance, when rounding a long curve at high speeds, the weight is thrown outward to the outer springs and lessens on the

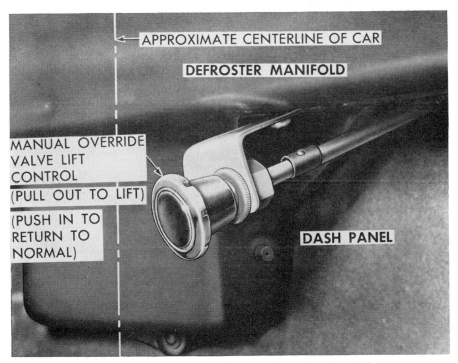

Fig. 125. Manual override valve lift control.

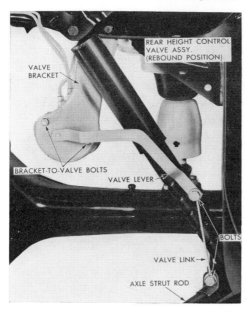

FIG. 126. Details of rear height control valve assembly.

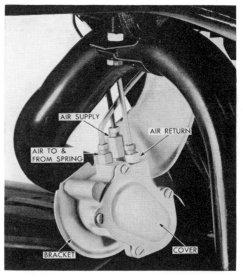

FIG. 127. Location of air lines to rear height control valve assembly.

inner springs. The height valves would level the car if some assistance were not available, and then would have to retrim after the turn had been made. The return flow orifice gives this assistance by holding the pressure in the exhaust lines for a limited time whenever a height control valve exhausts air. This back pressure slows down flow through the exhaust valves during turning, braking, and accelerating, thereby greatly reducing undesirable trimming.

SERVICE PROCEDURES

Jack Instructions. The manual lift knob must be pulled out so the car is in the fully *raised* position before using a bumper jack to raise the car. After the jacking operation is completed, the manual lift knob must be pushed back firmly into the *normal operating position* before the car is driven.

Height Control Valve Removal, Typical:

CAUTION: *Never force any height control valve lever against its stop in either direction; this would bend the inner valve operating lever and throw off the valve setting.*

Removal:

1. Exhaust all air at the drain petcock on the air tank.
2. Jack up the front of the car at the center of the spring cross member.
3. Place floor stands under the front of the frame side rails and remove the jack.
4. Disconnect the height valve link at the clamp bracket on the stabilizer bar.
5. Remove the front spring cross member lower cover
6. Disconnect all air lines at the height valve allowing the cross flow control tee to remain with the air lines.
7. Remove the two valve bracket mounting bolts at the front of the cross member, and then remove the bracket and valve assembly.
8. Remove the bracket from the height valve.

Replacement:

1. Reverse steps 8 through 6 used in removal. Use new "O"-rings at all air line fittings.
2. Before replacing the spring cross member lower cover:
   a. Fill the air tank at the filler fitting with available air pressure.
   b. Operate the height valve link slightly to pressurize the front springs.
3. Use a bubble solution at air line connections on height valve to check for leaks.
4. Reverse steps 5 through 1 in removal.
5. Check the valve operation by applying weight to the front bumper.

Fig. 128. Details of compressor and its mounting.

Air Compressor—Power Steering Pump, Removal and Replacement:

Removal:

1. Exhaust air out of the air tank at the drain petcock.
2. Loosen the vented pulley nut and remove it.
3. Remove the compressor belt and pulley.
4. Disconnect the power steering pump hoses.
5. Remove the air inlet tee at the compressor.
6. Remove the high pressure hose and check the valve at the compressor.
7. Disconnect the compressor-pump assembly from its brackets and remove it from the car.
8. Remove the oil from the reservoir.
9. Remove the two compressor-to-pump bolts. Unless the pump seal is to be replaced, install two guide pins in the compressor to avoid damage to the seal. Separate the compressor from the pump.

Replacement:

1. Install two guide pins in the compressor.
2. Carefully align the pump on the guide pins to avoid damage to the seal and push it into contact with the compressor. Remove the pins and install two compressor-to-pump bolts. Tighten to 25–30 ft. lbs. torque.

3. Mount the compressor-pump assembly in the brackets. Install, but do not tighten the bolts.

4. Connect the high pressure hose and check the valve to the compressor.

5. Connect the inlet tee at the compressor.

6. Connect the power steering hoses to the pump.

7. Install the compressor pulley and belt. Securely tighten the vented pulley nut.

8. Adjust the belt tension and tighten the mounting bolts. Tension should be 30 to 35 ft. lbs. torque on pulley nut to slip old belt (40 to 45 ft. lbs. torque to slip new belt).

9. Fill the reservoir to the proper level with specified oil. Run the engine and check for leaks. Do not remove the reservoir cover when engine is running above idle speed.

CAUTION: *Since the compressor is dependent on the power steering oil pump for lubrication, it is most important that the reservoir oil level be at the full mark at all times. After replacing the compressor-pump assembly and running the engine, check the oil level with the engine idling and add oil as needed. Also check the compressor oil pump by observing the flow at the oil return standpipe.*

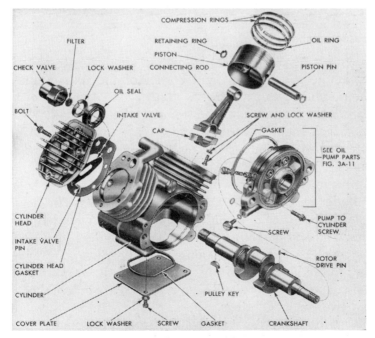

Fig. 129. Exploded view of compressor.

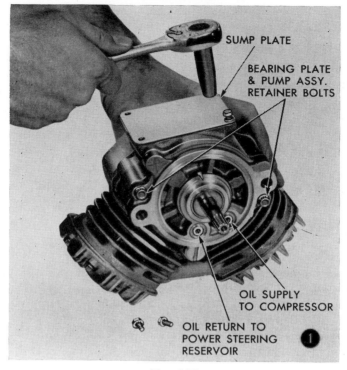

SUMP PLATE

BEARING PLATE & PUMP ASSY. RETAINER BOLTS

OIL SUPPLY TO COMPRESSOR

OIL RETURN TO POWER STEERING RESERVOIR

Fig. 130

Compressor Repair:

Disassembly. Each of the following steps is illustrated. The number in the lower right hand corner of the illustration agrees with the numbered steps below.

1. Invert the compressor and remove the four bolts and lock washers which retain the sump cover plate to the block. Remove the plate and square-cut rubber sealing ring. Allow all of the oil to drain out.

2. Turn the compressor over and remove the six head bolts from each cylinder head. Remove the heads and gaskets. The heads may be tapped lightly with a rawhide mallet to break them loose. Do not pry. Scrape off any gasket material remaining on the heads or block.

3. Remove the two bolts retaining the bearing plate and pump assembly to the block. Carefully slide it from the crankshaft to prevent damaging the bearing. Remove the square-cut rubber sealing ring and two small "O" rings.

4. Invert the compressor and work through the sump opening to remove the rod bolts, lock washers, and caps.

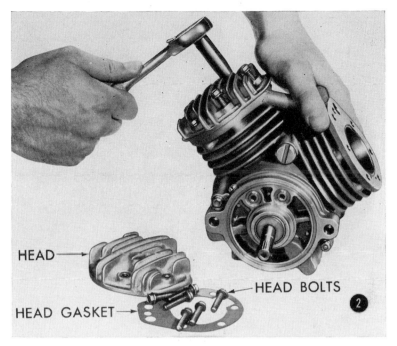

HEAD

HEAD BOLTS

HEAD GASKET

Fig. 131

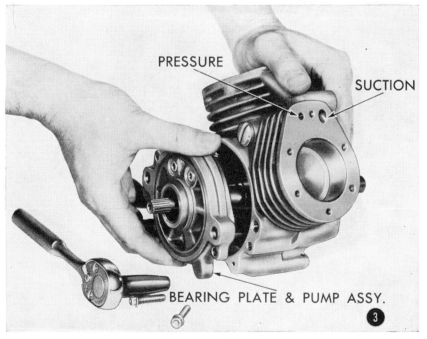

PRESSURE

SUCTION

BEARING PLATE & PUMP ASSY.

Fig. 132

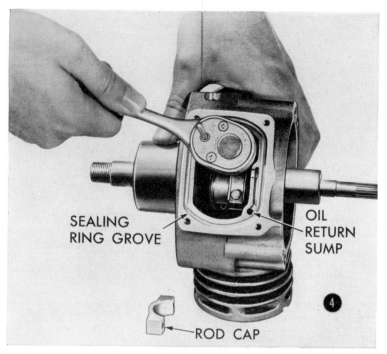

FIG. 133

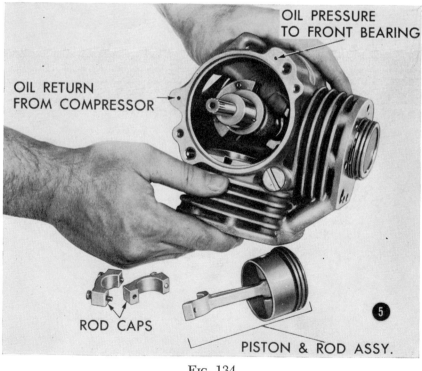

FIG. 134

FIG. 135

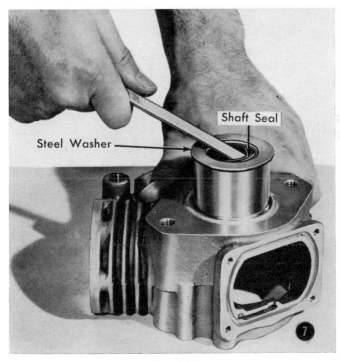

FIG. 136

93

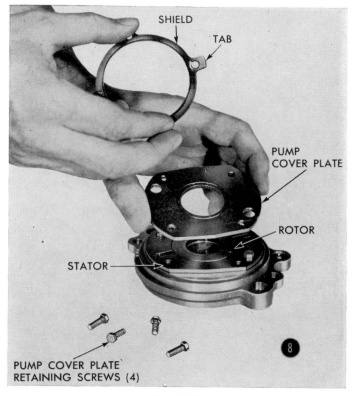

FIG. 137

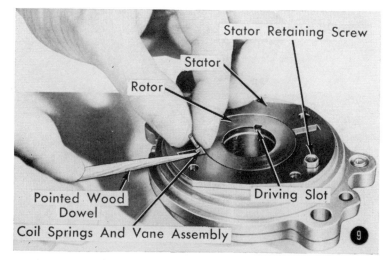

FIG. 138

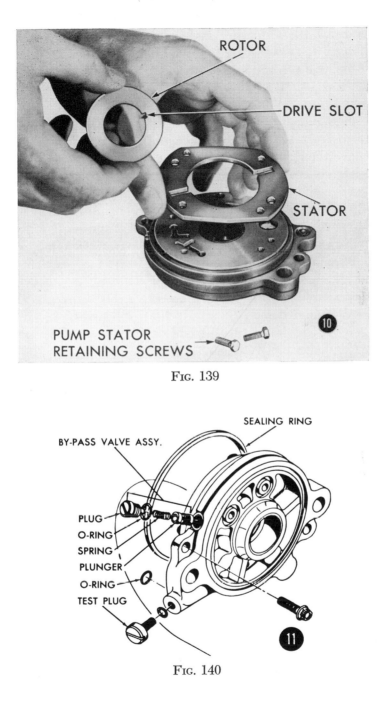

ROTOR

DRIVE SLOT

STATOR

PUMP STATOR
RETAINING SCREWS

10

FIG. 139

SEALING RING

BY-PASS VALVE ASSY.

PLUG

O-RING

SPRING

PLUNGER

O-RING

TEST PLUG

11

FIG. 140

5. Push the pistons and rods out of the bores. Remove the piston pin snap rings, the piston pin, and the piston rings.

6. Remove the crankshaft from the block through the rear.

7. To remove the crankshaft oil seal, place a steel washer around the outer face of the seal opening to protect the bore. Insert the tip of a screwdriver well into the rubber seal to insure contact with the metal flange and pry upward.

8. To disassemble the pump assembly, bend the lock tabs flat and remove the four retaining screws. Remove the pump shield and cover plate.

9. Remove the two coil spring and vane assemblies.

10. Remove the rotor and stator.

11. Remove the by-pass valve plug, spring, and plunger.

Cleaning and Inspecting. Wash all metal parts in a suitable solvent and blow them dry with compressed air. Inspect all parts for wear. See that all openings and passageways are clean. Replace the complete piston assembly if any part is defective. The crankshaft journal must measure between 0.999″ and 1.000″. Inspect the front seal bore for roughness which must be dressed down before installing a new seal.

Assembling. (In general, the assembly is the reverse of disassembly, therefore, only the especially important steps are illustrated.)

12. Install a new seal flush with the top of the bore. Lubricate the seal and install the crankshaft. Before replacing the rings, check their end gaps as follows: Compression and scraper rings should be between 0.002″ and 0.007″, and the oil ring should have between 0.005″ and 0.013″ clearance. Install the rings on the pistons with the raised dot on each ring in an *up* position. Stagger the ring gaps 120° apart. Care must be exercised when installing the two upper rings that the correct ring is used in each groove. The rings and grooves vary in depth.

13. Install the assembly into the bore with the long ear of the connecting rod toward the top of the block. Attach the rod cap. The grooves on one side of the rod and cap must match. Tighten the rod bolts to 25–30 *inch* pounds torque. Clean the sump oil return line filter screen and install it. Place a new square-cut rubber sealing ring in the channel around the sump opening. Replace the sump cover plate and tighten it to 40–50 *inch* pounds torque.

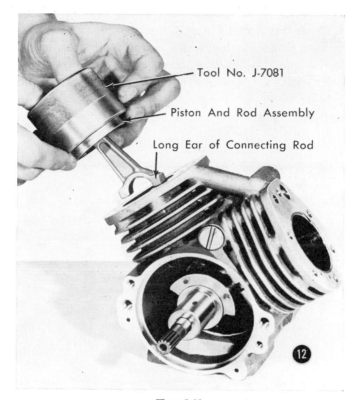

Tool No. J-7081

Piston And Rod Assembly

Long Ear of Connecting Rod

Fig. 141

CRANKSHAFT
SPLINES

Fig. 142

14. Install a new head gasket on the block using a few drops of oil to hold it in position. Do not use sealer or cement. Be sure the intake (suction) valve is located correctly over the dowel pins on the head. Replace the head being careful to align the dowel pins with the matching holes in the cylinder block. Install and tighten the head bolts to 80–90 *inch* pounds torque. Alternately tighten from side to side to insure a good seal.

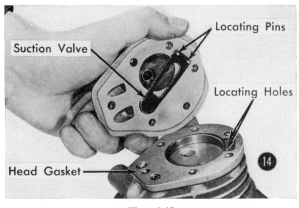

Fig. 143

15. To assemble the pump, replace the test plug using a new "O" ring. Replace the by-pass valve plunger, spring, and plug using a new "O" ring. Position the pump stator on the bearing plate with the six mounting holes aligned. Install the two stator retaining screws finger-tight.

16. Place the stator alignment tool in the stator cavity. The tool must be clean and free of oil. Work the aligning tool and bearing plate very carefully onto the crankshaft to prevent damaging the bearing journal. Do not use force. With the stator in position where the aligning tool and bearing plate rotate freely, tighten the two retaining screws.

Recheck the stator alignment by removing the bearing plate from the crankshaft, revolving the aligning tool 90°, and again placing it on the crankshaft. The aligning tool should rotate freely on the crankshaft and in the pump stator. If it does not rotate freely, loosen the stator retaining screws and repeat the alignment procedure.

17. Remove the stator aligning tool and install the rotor. Install new pump vanes and springs. Lubricate the pump and replace the pump cover plate and shield. Insert the four retaining screws and

FIG. 144

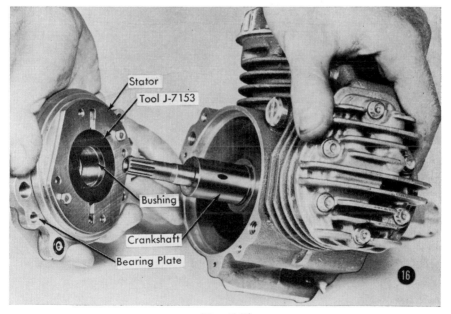

FIG. 145

tighten them to 25–30 *inch* pounds torque. Bend the tabs to lock the bolts. Install the bearing plate and pump assembly. Be sure that the drive pin enters the slot in the rotor. Rotate the bearing plate back and forth slightly until it does, and then press the assembly forward. Tighten the retaining bolts to 40–50 *inch* pounds torque.

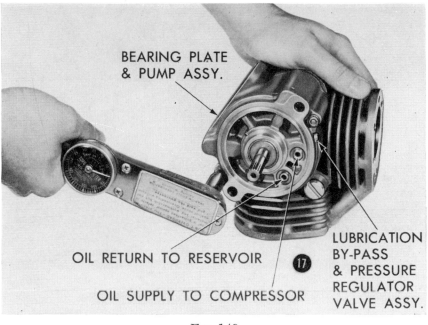

BEARING PLATE
& PUMP ASSY.

LUBRICATION
BY-PASS
& PRESSURE
REGULATOR
VALVE ASSY.

OIL RETURN TO RESERVOIR

OIL SUPPLY TO COMPRESSOR

FIG. 146

Height Control Valve Repair:

Disassembling. Each of the following steps is illustrated. The number in the lower right hand corner of the illustration agrees with the numbered steps below.

CAUTION: *Removal of either valve core requires that it be adjusted after assembly.*

1. Remove the cover plate and discard the "O" ring. Remove the intake, exhaust, and air spring adapters and discard the three "O" rings, intake screen, and the three square-cut adapter gaskets.

2. Remove the two dash pot retainer screws and carefully disengage the dash pot shaft from the slot of the valve actuating arm. Rotate the dash pot slightly clockwise to remove it. Be careful not to damage the stem of the exhaust valve. If the exhaust valve is to be replaced, clip off the valve stem as shown.

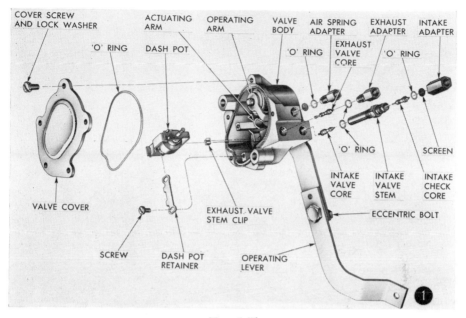

FIG. 147

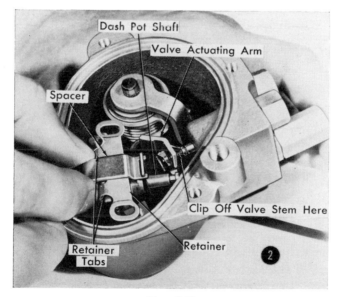

FIG. 148

3. To replace a defective exhaust valve core, use a valve removing tool as shown.

4. To replace an intake valve core, remove the assembly and discard the "O" ring. Using the valve removing tool, remove both valve cores from the intake valve stem assembly. (The intake check valve core is the shorter of the two and is located in the hex head end of the stem assembly.)

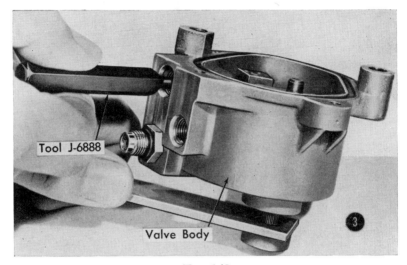

Fig. 149

Cleaning and Inspecting. Clean all parts with solvent. Dry with low-pressure air (25 psi max.) Inspect all parts for defects and replace any that are needed.

Assembling. (The assembly is the reverse of disassembly and, therefore, no illustrations are needed.)

Install both intake valve cores in the stem assembly and tighten them to 2½ to 3 *inch* pounds torque. Install new "O" rings and the intake valve stem into the valve body. Tighten it to 12–15 *inch* pounds torque.

Install the exhaust valve core and tighten it to 2½ to 3 *inch* pounds torque. Spread the ears of the exhaust valve stem clip and place it on the valve stem between the head and the arm tab. Carefully brace the valve stem to prevent damage. Pinch the ears of the clip together so that it is retained on the stem. Do not pinch the clip too tightly as it must rotate freely on the stem.

Place a new "O" ring and square-cut gasket on each of the three adapters and install them in the valve body. Tighten each to 12–15 *inch* pounds torque.

Insert the retainer between the dash pot body and the spacer with the two retainer tabs away from the dash pot shaft. Place the dash pot into the valve body and engage the recess of the dash pot shaft in the slot of the valve actuating arm. The retainer tabs must hold the dash pot firmly against the two shoulders of the valve body

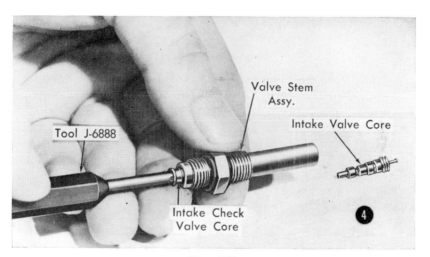

Fig. 150

recess. If necessary, manually operate the lever assembly slightly to allow the dash pot body to seat against the shoulders. Recheck the dash pot installation by manually operating the lever. The dash pot body must not move.

Adjusting. (The exact point of opening of the valves must be adjusted if either one has been replaced. If only the intake check valve core has been replaced, no adjustment is needed.)

5. Connect a test hose to an air pressure line and reduce the line pressure to 10–20 psi. Install the other end of the test hose to the air return exhaust fitting and tighten it. Place the 0.049″ side of the gauge between the operating lever stop and the middle ear of the operating lever. Insert the wedge gauge between the other side of the stop and the lever ear and press down securely. The wedge gauge should hold the feeler gauge so that it does not fall out. Using a suitable tool, such as a thin-blade screwdriver, and moderately

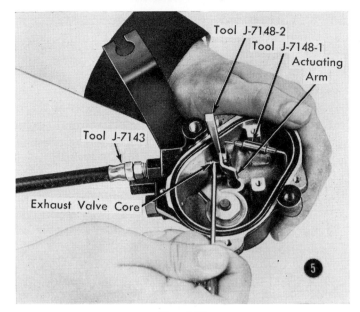

FIG. 151

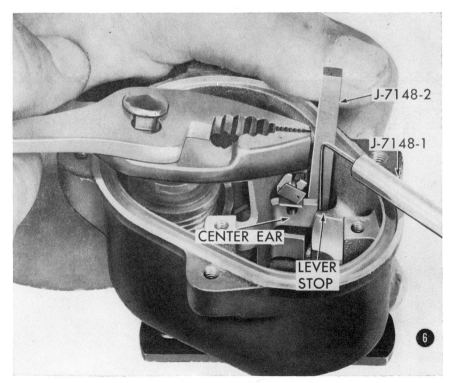

FIG. 152

light pressure, press against the exhaust core at the core seal seat. A slight amount of air leakage should be heard. Insert the 0.053″ end of the gauge between the stop and the center ear of the operating lever, and repeat the operation. The valve must seal completely, and no air should be heard.

6. If air leakage was heard during the 0.053″ test, bend the upper ear of the operating lever slightly toward the valve core seal. Use the screwdriver to press in and seal the core seat. If the bending was

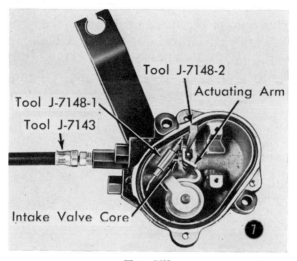

Fig. 153

sufficient, no air leakage should be heard. If leakage is still heard, then the upper ear was not moved enough. If no leakage is heard, remove the gauges and repeat the test using the 0.049″ end of the gauge. A slight amount of leakage should be heard.

7. To adjust the intake valve, place the 0.049″ end of the gauge between the side of the lever stop nearest to the valve cores and the middle ear of the operating lever and insert the wedge gauge on the opposite side. Install the test hose on the inlet fitting. Increase the line pressure to 50–80 psi. A slight amount of air leakage should be heard. If not, bend the lower ear toward the intake valve core until some leakage is heard. Place the 0.053″ end of the gauge in the same location and install the wedge gauge. No air leakage should be heard. If air leakage does exist, bend the lower ear away from the valve core just enough to stop all air leakage. Recheck using the 0.049″ end of the gauge.

Manual Override Valve Repair:

Disassembling. Each of the following steps is illustrated. The number in the lower right hand corner of the illustration agrees with the numbered steps below.

1. Remove the lever spring from the bracket and manual lever and remove the dust boot. Remove the three screws holding the Bowden control wire bracket and remove the bracket. Remove the fourth screw from the pressure regulator housing and remove the housing. *Measure and record the distance that the regulator adjusting screw extends from the housing.* Remove the regulator spring and piston. Remove and discard the regulator diaphragm.

2. Remove the intake filter retainer and "O" ring. Use a tool to remove the intake valve stem assembly. Remove the retainer spring and discard the retainer. Remove the exhaust silencer fitting. Remove the spring and plate. The hexagonal plunger will drop out after the camshaft is removed.

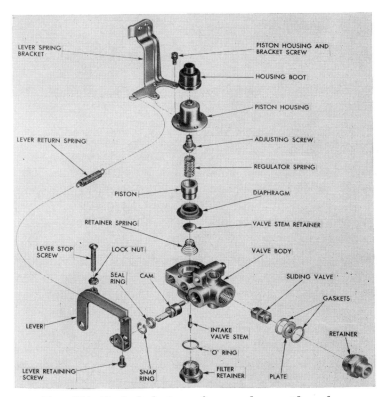

Fig. 154. Exploded view of manual override valve.

3. Using snap ring pliers, remove the retaining ring and the camshaft. Now remove the hexagonal plunger.

Cleaning and Inspecting. Clean all parts with solvent. Blow dry with air pressure. The seal on the valve stem, and the other rubber

Fig. 155

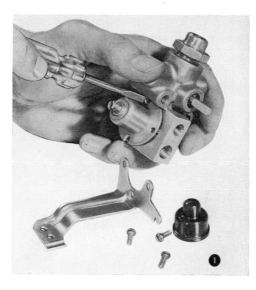

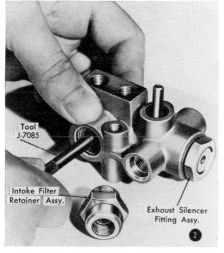

Fig. 156

parts, are very critical, therefore, they should be replaced. Replace any other part that seems doubtful.

Assembling. (The assembly is the reverse of disassembly, therefore, no illustrations are needed.)

Insert the hexagonal plunger in the valve body with the groove located to receive the cam. Place a new "O" ring on the cam and install it with the pin matching with the groove in the hexagonal plunger. The flat side of the camshaft should be *up*. Lock the camshaft with the snap ring. Install the manual lever on the camshaft and secure it with a setscrew.

Install new gaskets at both sides of the seat plate. Install the spring and a new screen. Tighten the exhaust control retainer in the valve body to complete this assembly.

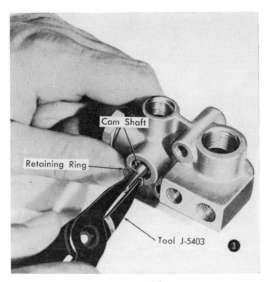

Fɪɢ. 157

Install a new valve stem in the lower cavity of the body and install the retainer spring and retainer in the upper cavity. Turn the stem clockwise while holding the stem retainer stationary with a No. 1 Truarc pliers. Tighten securely.

Install the filter retainer and a new diaphragm, being careful to center it. Install the adjusting screw in the housing. Allow the screw to extend out at the top the same distance as was measured on removal. Position the regulator spring in the housing against the adjusting screw. Install the piston over the regulator spring. Install the housing assembly and the bracket on the valve body. The edge of the diaphragm must show evenly in all four holes of the housing, or the diaphragm is not centered. Install the four screws and tighten them securely.

Install the return spring on the bracket and manual lever. Install the dust boot over the housing.

After installing the manual override valve on the car, it must be adjusted for the correct line pressure.

Checking and Setting Supply Line Pressure:

1. Bring the air tank pressure up to 200 psi minimum.

2. Disconnect the air return line on the top of the manual override valve and install a test hose in the valve fitting.

3. Pull the manual lift knob to put the car into the *lift* position.

4. Press the test gauge onto the test hose and take a reading. Remove the gauge.

5. If the pressure is more than 145 psi, remove the boot from the override valve and turn the adjusting screw out (counterclockwise) ½ turn at a time.

6. Depress the Schrader core in the end of the hose for five seconds and then take another gauge reading.

7. If the reading is still too high, repeat the procedure until the correct reading is obtained. If the valve cannot be adjusted, remove the valve and disassemble.

8. If the pressure is less than 135 psi, turn the pressure adjusting screw in (clockwise) ½ turn and then take a gauge reading. Repeat the procedure until the correct reading is obtained.

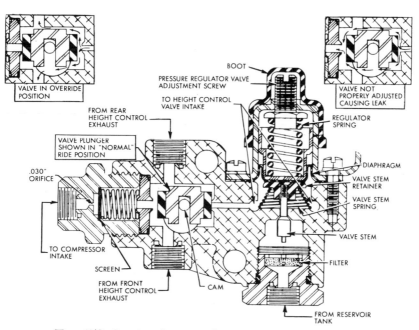

Fig. 158. Sectional view of manual override valve.

Note: Any time an override valve is to be disassembled, measure the height of the pressure adjusting screw that extends out of the housing. Then, after assembling, position the screw at the same height and follow the procedure for checking and setting the supply line pressure.

9. Push the manual lift knob all the way *in* to lower the car to normal trim height.

10. Depress the Schrader core in the hose to exhaust all air from the test hose, and then remove the hose.

11. Connect the air return line at the override valve using a new sealing ring, and pull the manual lift knob to put the car into the *lift* position. Use a bubble solution at the fitting connection to check for leaks. Push the knob *in* to lower the car.

CONTROL WIRE SHEATH CLAMP

LIFT LEVER STOP SCREW

1/8" MAX. FREE MOVEMENT

SCREW AGAINST STOP

REAR HEIGHT VALVE SUPPLY

SPRING LOADED CONNECTOR

FROM RESERVOIR TANK

REAR HEIGHT VALVE EXHAUST

EXHAUST TO COMPRESSOR INTAKE

FRONT HEIGHT VALVE SUPPLY

FRONT HEIGHT VALVE EXHAUST

OVERRIDE PRESSURE RELIEF VALVE

MANUAL OVERRIDE VALVE IN NORMAL RIDE POSITION

Fig. 159. Manual override control cable adjustment.

Checking and Adjusting the Manual Override Valve Control Cable. If the manual override valve control cable is not in proper adjustment, the override plunger may not seat when the control knob is in the *normal ride* position and a constant air leak will result. Also, when the control knob is in the *override* position, incorrect adjustment may prevent the plunger from seating, resulting in an air leak. Check the control cable adjustments as follows:

1. Make sure the override control knob is pushed *in* fully.

2. On the manual override valve, grasp the control lever stop screw and lift the lever slightly. If the control cable is properly adjusted, the lever should have a slight amount of free motion, but not over ⅛".

3. To adjust the override valve control cable, loosen the conduit clamp screw.

4. Slide the conduit fully down and then raise it about ¹⁄₁₆".

5. Tighten the conduit clamp screw and recheck the adjustment.

Checking and Adjusting the Manual Override Lever Stopscrew. The control lever stopscrew setting should never be changed without first checking the control cable adjustment as described above. If the stopscrew is against its stop and there is still an air leak past the override plunger, try adjusting the stopscrew as follows:

1. Note the position of the screw. Then loosen the locknut and back out the screw just until the air stops leaking. (If backing the screw out does not stop the air leak, the stopscrew was not out of adjustment. Return the screw to its original setting and look elsewhere for the trouble.)

2. Now back out the screw exactly two turns from this point and tighten the locknut.

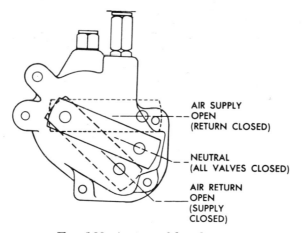

AIR SUPPLY
OPEN
(RETURN CLOSED)

NEUTRAL
(ALL VALVES CLOSED)

AIR RETURN
OPEN
(SUPPLY
CLOSED)

Fig. 160. Action of height arm.

Checking and Setting Trim Heights:

1. Check the operation of the height control valves by applying weight to each side of the rear bumper, one side at a time, and to the center of the front bumper. The car should raise back to normal trim height after weight has been added and should lower to the proper height after the weight has been removed.

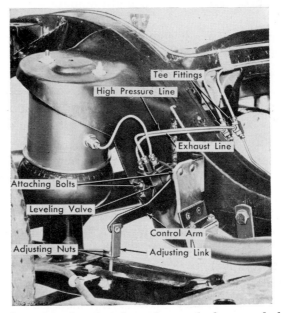

FIG. 161. To adjust trim height of car, loosen locknut and slide adjusting link back and forth until measurement is at specified height. Then lock locknut.

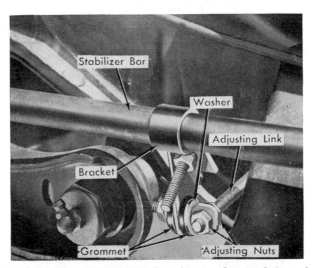

FIG. 162. Front leveling adjusting link is fastened to stabilizer bar. Adjustment is made in same way as that of rear links.

2. Check and correct tire pressures and inspect for any binding anywhere in the suspension system. Correct if necessary.

3. Check shock absorber action by comparing its action with that of a known good shock absorber.

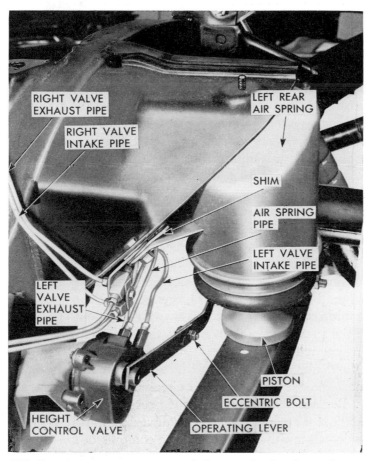

RIGHT VALVE EXHAUST PIPE

RIGHT VALVE INTAKE PIPE

LEFT REAR AIR SPRING

SHIM

AIR SPRING PIPE

LEFT VALVE INTAKE PIPE

LEFT VALVE EXHAUST PIPE

PISTON

ECCENTRIC BOLT

HEIGHT CONTROL VALVE

OPERATING LEVER

FIG. 163. Pontiac uses an eccentric bolt to make leveling adjustment.

4. There is a "neutral zone" in every height control valve; that is, a dead spot where some movement of the height valve arm is possible without opening either the exhaust or intake valve. To eliminate the variation in trim height caused by this "neutral zone," always manually trim the car by pulling down on the frame until air enters the air spring. Then gradually release the downward pull, allowing the car to retrim.

5. Check the trim heights against specifications.

6. If trim heights are not correct, loosen the two bracket-to-height valve screws on the front side of each bracket, and rotate the height valve in the correct direction. The holes in the brackets are elongated to allow for valve rotation.

TROUBLESHOOTING

The oil pump pressure may be checked accurately by removing the test plug, connecting a suitable pressure gauge, and running the engine at idle.

A satisfactory test may be made by removing the reservoir cover with the engine idling. The oil return standpipe should have oil and air welling out. Observing the action at this standpipe in a known good job will give a standard for comparison. Never run the engine faster than idle speed while the cover is removed or oil will spray over the engine compartment.

Compressor Test. Check the air tank pressure. If the tank pressure is generally low, make a compressor output check as follows:

1. Start the engine and set the speed at 1500 rpm.

2. Check the air pressure at the upper air tank fitting. If the pressure is over 150 psi, release air until the pressure is below 150 psi.

3. When the gauge hits 150 psi, start timing the compressor. Pressure should rise from 150 psi to 200 psi in 2½ minutes or less.

4. If the pressure does not rise at the specified rate, compressor pumping capacity is low. Check for a clogged suction hose or pipe. Check for leaks in the high pressure hoses or fittings. If they are okay, next remove the heads and check each reed valve for proper seating. Replace the intake valves if necessary. If an exhaust valve is defective, the complete head and valve assembly must be replaced.

If no defective valves are found, the compressor must be removed and overhauled.

Air Leak Checking Procedure. An internal leak is caused either by the manual override valve losing air from the pressure to the exhaust side (past the override valve plunger) or by one or more of the height valve exhaust cores leaking. Check for an internal leak as follows:

1. Make sure the manual lift control knob is pushed *in* fully. With the car at trim height and the engine not running, disconnect the return hose at the compressor inlet tee and use a bubble solution in the end of the hose. **Note:** This must be done without any weight change on the car. If weight is added, such as by leaning on a fender,

Fig. 164. Hooking up a pressure gauge to compressor to check output pressure.

and then removed, the height valves would automatically exhaust air.

2. If the hose does not blow bubbles, there are no internal leaks. Proceed to check for external leaks.

3. If the hose blows bubbles, make sure that the manual override control wire is correctly adjusted so that the stopscrew on the override lever is against the stop (lever in full *down* position). Then recheck for a leak at the exhaust hose, making sure no car weight change takes place while checking.

4. If the return system still leaks, disconnect the air return line at each height valve and use the bubble solution on the exhaust fittings (exhaust fitting is the short fitting nearest the cover plate). If an exhaust core leaks, the height control valve must be removed from the car for repair and internal adjustment.

5. If the exhaust valve cores in all height valves are okay, but return system still leaks, the manual override valve seat is leaking. Try backing out the override lever stopscrew slightly; if leaking still continues, the override valve must be removed for repair.

6. If the internal system is free of leaks, check for external leaks by applying the bubble solution to all joints and fittings. Correct any leaks found.

TROUBLESHOOTING CHART

TROUBLES	CAUSES
1. One side of car higher than trim height	1a. Rear height valve improperly adjusted.
	1b. Plugged orifice or screen in one rear height valve exhaust fitting.
	1c. Inoperative exhaust valve in one rear height valve.
2. Front of car higher than trim height	2a. Front height valve improperly adjusted.
	2b. Plugged orifice or screen in front height valve exhaust fitting.
	2c. Inoperative exhaust valve in front height valve.
3. Whole car higher than trim height or car fails to trim after manual override setting is used	3a. Manual override valve exhaust screen or orifice plugged.
	3b. Manual override valve not adjusted properly.
4. One side of car lower than trim height with minimum of 150 psi tank pressure	4a. Rear height valve not adjusted properly.
	4b. Plugged intake valve orifice or screen in rear height valve.
	4c. Inoperative intake valve in rear height valve.
5. Front of car lower than trim height with minimum of 150 psi tank pressure	5a. Front height valve not properly adjusted.
	5b. Plugged intake valve orifice or screen in front height valve.
	5c. Inoperative intake valve in front height valve.
	5d. Pressure regulator valve in manual override valve adjusted too low.
6. Loss of tank pressure and car settles on one side while parked	6a. Leak at rear air spring, height valve, or line connecting valve to spring.
7. Loss of tank pressure and car settles in front while parked	7a. Leak at front air spring, height valve, or connecting lines. NOTE:If there is a supply system leak and tank pressure falls, due to the normally greater weight on the front of the car, the front intake check valve may leak back through the supply line and allow the front of the car to settle.

TROUBLESHOOTING CHART—(Continued)

TROUBLES	CAUSES
8. Loss of tank pressure but car stays at trim height while parked	8a. Leak at compressor check valve.
	8b. Leaking intake valve core allowing a supply leak into an air spring which raises the car above trim height causing the exhaust valve to open and re-trim the car. Repetition of the cycle lowers the tank pressure to the air spring pressure.
	8c. Leak at the tank, fittings, or supply lines.
9. Poor handling while driving (car rolls excessively)	9a. Cross flow control tee not restricting flow of air from one front spring to the other.

REVIEW QUESTIONS

1. In what way does the air suspension system differ from a steel spring suspension?
2. What is the operating pressure at the storage tank?
3. Why is it necessary to provide a control button to be used by the driver to overrule the air suspension system at certain times?
4. For what purpose is the Schrader-type air valve used in the air tank?
5. What is the normal pressure within the air springs?
6. To what operating pressure does the manual override valve regulate the high pressure coming from the storage tank?
7. To what height will the height control valves allow the car to be raised?
8. How many height control valves are used?
9. What is the "dwell" period built into the height control valves?
10. What is the purpose of the cross flow control tee?
11. Why is some back pressure retained in the exhaust lines?
12. What caution is given with regard to forcing a height control valve lever against its stop?
13. What caution is given in regard to the compressor lubrication when the compressor is replaced?
14. When repairing the compressor, what is the purpose of the stator alignment tool?
15. What caution is given regarding the removal of a valve core when disassembling the height control valve?
16. To what operating pressure is the test air line adjusted when testing the operation of the height control valves?
17. Why is it necessary to measure the distance the regulator adjusting screw extends from the manual override valve housing before removing it?

18. After installing the manual override valve on the car, how is it adjusted for the correct line pressure?
19. What is the operating result if the manual override control cable is not in proper adjustment?
20. How can you check the operation of the height control valves?
21. How is the trim height adjusted?
22. What suggestion is given for testing the oil pump pressure?
23. How long should it take a good compressor to raise the pressure from 150 psi to 200 psi?

4

BODY POWER MECHANISMS

Power mechanisms discussed in this chapter are power tops, seats, and windows.

RETRACTABLE HARDTOP
THEORY OF OPERATION

The hardtop has a complete steel roof assembly which may be lowered into the luggage compartment. The entire cycle is completely automatic and is accomplished through electric motor powered mechanical linkage.

The deck lid and roof linkage are driven by electric motors through flexible drive shafts which are attached to screw jacks. Assisting springs are attached to the linkage to aid in the opening of the deck

FIG. 165 (*top*). The hardtop with the top up.

FIG. 166 (*bottom*). The hardtop with the top retracted into the rear deck area.

119

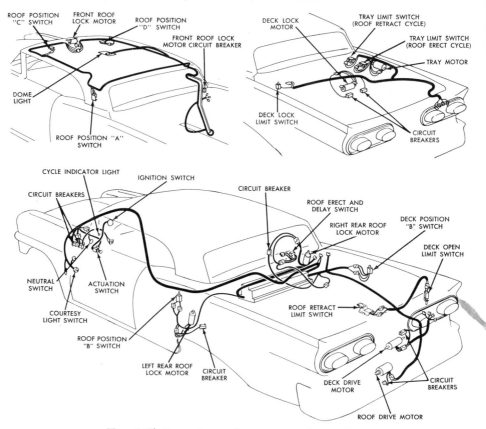

FIG. 167. Locations of motors and switches.

lid and to smooth out the final motion of the roof as it is lowered into the luggage compartment.

The electrical system includes seven reversible motors, ten power relays, eleven limit switches, an actuating switch, a neutral switch, and a cycle indicator light which is actuated by the deck lid unlocking mechanism. The electrical system is protected by a circuit breaker in the control circuit feed, a common motor feed circuit breaker, and an individual circuit breaker in each motor ground feed.

When the ignition switch is turned to the ON or ACC position, power is available through the circuit breaker to the vehicle motion interlock switch. The interlock, or neutral switch, is *open* when the gearshift lever is in any position other than *neutral.* With the transmission in *neutral,* power is available at the roof actuating switch. This is a standard spring loaded switch that returns to the center, or *neutral* position, when released. When the switch is pulled *out* and held, the roof will retract. When the switch is pushed *in* and held, the roof will erect. If the switch is released at any point, all motion stops. The direction of motion may be reversed at any point without completing the cycle by actuating the switch in the opposite direction.

The operating principles of the retractable roof will be divided into two cycles, a *retract* cycle and an *erect* cycle. Each cycle will be broken down further to simplify the explanation.

Retract Cycle. This cycle starts with the roof in the *erect* position with the deck lid closed and locked.

Deck Lid Unlock. With the actuation switch in the *retract* position, current flows through the roof erect and delay switch, the deck open limit switch, and the deck unlock power relay to actuate the deck lock motor. The motor, through two flexible drive shafts, unlocks the deck lid.

Deck Lid Opening. The mechanical motion of unlocking the deck lid actuates the deck position "B" switch and the deck lock limit switch. Actuating these two switches allows current to flow to the cycle indicator light. Further actuation of the deck position "B" switch allows current to flow to the deck open power relay to actuate the deck motor. The deck motor raises the deck lid. When the lid reaches the *open* position, the mechanical motion of the deck actuates the deck open limit switch which stops the deck lock motor and the deck motor.

Package Tray Extend. The actuation of the deck open limit switch by the deck, which opens the deck motor and the deck lock motor circuits, also closes a second set of contacts in the deck open limit switch. Closing this set of contacts allows current to flow through the tray limit switch to the tray power relay actuating the tray motor and extending the package tray so that it is parallel with the deck lid. The mechanical action of the tray, as it reaches the parallel position, opens the tray limit switch which stops the tray motor.

Roof Unlock. When the tray limit switch is opened by the action of the package tray, another set of contacts in the tray limit switch is closed. This allows current to flow through the roof position "A" switch to the roof unlock power relay, actuating the roof front lock motor and the two roof rear lock motors. The motors drive power locks, two at the header and one at each roof quarter, to unlock the roof.

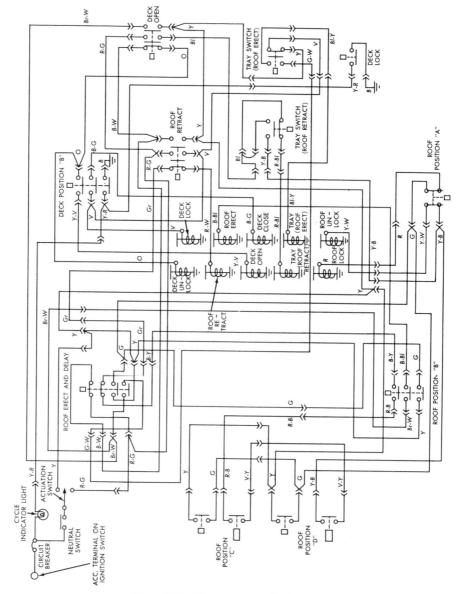

Fig. 168. Motor control circuits.

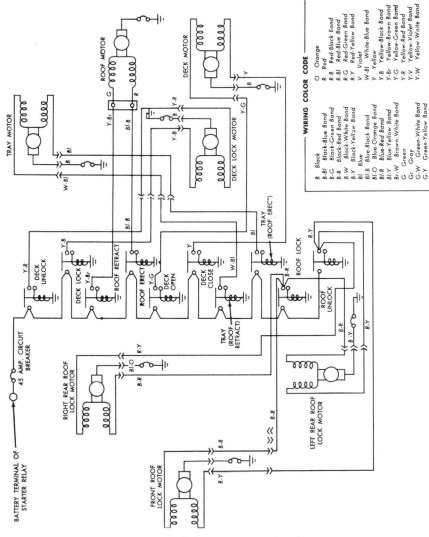

Fig. 169. Motor power circuits.

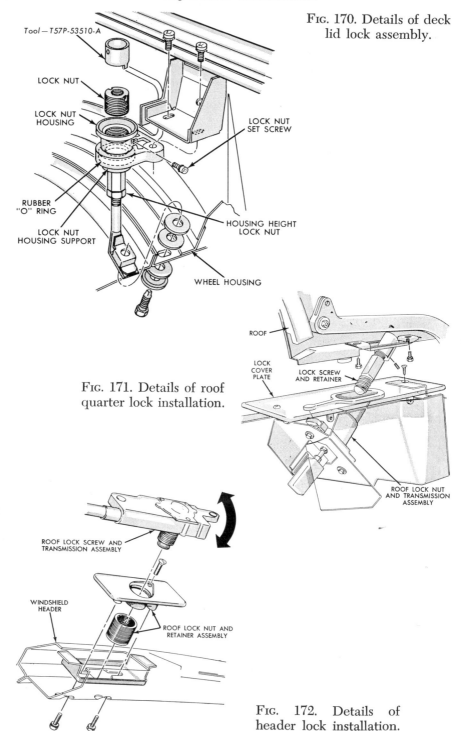

Tool — T57P-53510-A

LOCK NUT

LOCK NUT
HOUSING

LOCK NUT
SET SCREW

RUBBER
"O" RING

LOCK NUT
HOUSING SUPPORT

HOUSING HEIGHT
LOCK NUT

WHEEL HOUSING

Fig. 170. Details of deck
lid lock assembly.

ROOF

LOCK
COVER
PLATE

LOCK SCREW
AND RETAINER

ROOF LOCK NUT
AND TRANSMISSION
ASSEMBLY

Fig. 171. Details of roof
quarter lock installation.

ROOF LOCK SCREW AND
TRANSMISSION ASSEMBLY

WINDSHIELD
HEADER

ROOF LOCK NUT AND
RETAINER ASSEMBLY

Fig. 172. Details of
header lock installation.

Roof Retract. As the roof is raised by the unlocking action of the four roof locks, the roof position "D" switch, and the roof erect and delay switch are actuated which allows current to flow through the roof retract limit switch to the roof retract power relay, actuating the roof motor. The roof motor retracts the roof. When the roof is raised about four inches off the locks, the rear roof left power link actuates the roof position "A" switch to stop the three roof lock motors. As the roof retracts, the front portion of the roof is folded

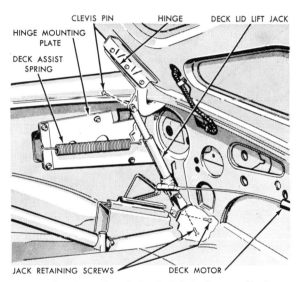

Fig. 173. Details of deck lid jack installation.

under the rear roof by means of mechanical linkage. When the roof reaches the fully retracted position, it actuates the roof retract limit switch to stop the roof motor.

Deck Lid Close and Lock. As the roof retract limit switch opens and stops the roof motor, another set of contacts, in the same switch, closes, allowing current to flow to the deck lock power relay through the deck position "B" switch to the deck close power relay to actuate the deck lid and deck lock motors. The deck motor then closes the deck lid. The deck lock motor locks the deck. As the deck lock screws draw the deck lid down, the deck position "B" switch is opened to stop the deck motor. When the deck is locked fully, the deck position "B" switch and the deck lock limit switch are actuated, turning off the cycle indicator light. When the cycle indicator light goes out, it shows that the deck lid is locked and that the actuation switch may be released to shut off the deck lock motor.

FIG. 174. Details of roof retract mechanism linkage.

Erect Cycle. This cycle starts with the roof in the luggage compartment and the deck lid closed and locked.

Deck Lid Unlock. With the actuation switch in the *erect* position, current flows through the roof retract limit switch, and the deck open limit switch, to the deck unlock power relay, actuating the deck lock motor. The motor drives the deck lock screws to unlock the deck lid.

Deck Lid Opening. The mechanical motion of unlocking the deck lid closes the deck position "B" switch (contacts farthest from the plunger), and the deck lock limit switch, allowing current to flow to the cycle indicator light. At the same time, the contacts closest to the plunger, of the deck position "B" switch, close to allow current to flow to the deck open power relay to actuate the deck motor.

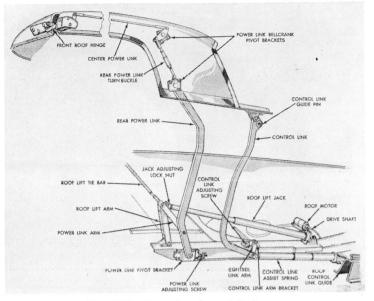

Fig. 175. Details of roof linkage.

The deck motor then raises the deck lid. As the deck lid reaches the fully *open* position, it opens the deck open limit switch (contacts closest to the plunger), stopping the deck lock motor and the deck motor.

Roof Erect. When the deck open limit switch opens, another set of contacts, in the same switch, *close* (contacts farthest from the plunger). This allows current to flow through the roof position "B" switch (middle contacts) to the roof erect power relay to actuate the roof motor. The motor then erects the roof. As the roof reaches the *erect* position, the middle contacts of the roof position "B" switch are opened and stop the roof motor.

Roof Lock. When the roof reaches a position approximately four inches above the roof locks, the roof position "A" switch *closes.* This allows current to flow through four paralleled switches to the roof lock power relay to actuate the three roof lock motors. When the left rear lock engages, it opens the roof position "B" switch middle contacts to stop the roof motor. The motion of the roof locking also opens the roof erect and delay switch (third set of contacts from the plunger), the roof position "C" switch, the roof position "D" switch, and the roof position "B" switch (contacts farthest from the plunger). When all four of these paralleled switches are opened, the roof lock power relay is de-energized to stop the three roof lock motors.

FIG. 176. Blocks of wood should be used to support roof to remove its weight from linkage when making adjustments.

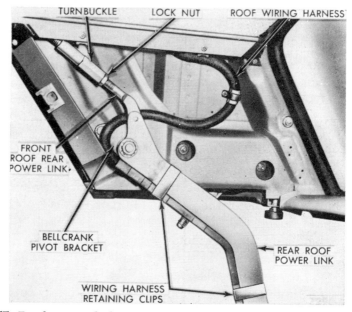

FIG. 177. Roof power links contain turnbuckles which may be adjusted so that continuity of surface between rear roof and front roof is achieved when front roof locking screws are 1 to 2 inches clear of locknuts in windshield header on roof erect cycle.

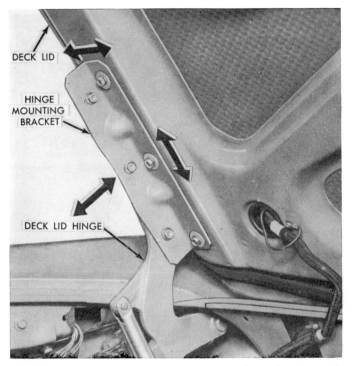

Fig. 178. Deck lid hinge adjustment is made with roof erect and package tray folded. Deck lid can be adjusted from side-to-side as well as fore-and-aft. Deck lid clearance and weatherstrip seal at rear roof and lower back panel are critical adjustment areas.

Package Tray Fold. As the roof reaches the *erect* position, it also *closes* the roof erect and delay switch (contacts farthest from the plunger), allowing current to flow through the tray limit switch to the tray power relay to actuate the tray motor. This motor folds the tray under the deck lid. When the tray is folded completely, the tray limit switch is opened to stop the tray motor.

Deck Lid Close and Lock. As the package tray is folded, a second set of contacts in the tray limit switch are closed, allowing current to flow to the deck lock power relay and also through the deck position "B" switch (middle contacts) to the deck close power relay. These two power relays actuate the deck lock motor and the deck motor to close and lock the deck lid. As the deck lid reaches the *closed* position, the deck position "B" switch (middle contacts) are opened to stop the deck motor. As the deck locks pull the deck lid to the *locked* position, the deck position "B" switch (contacts farthest

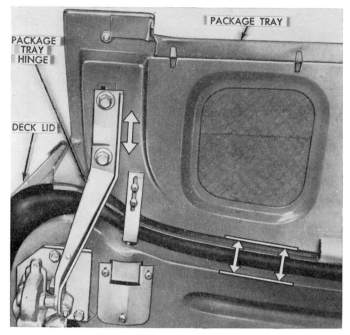

Fɪɢ. 179. Package tray adjustment is made to obtain proper clearance and seal between front edge of deck lid and tray.

from the plunger), and the deck lock limit switch are opened. This turns *off* the cycle indicator light and shows the operator that the cycle is complete and that the actuation switch may be released to stop the deck lock motor.

SERVICE PROCEDURES

Roof Adjustment. A roof adjustment is necessary whenever any component of the roof mechanical linkage is replaced or it becomes necessary to correct alignment. There are three basic adjustments: (1) the right and left power link adjustment which provides fore-and-aft as well as up-and-down adjustments; (2) the right and left control link adjustment which changes the height of the front of the roof while the rear remains practically constant; and (3) the roof lift jacks may be lengthened or shortened to move the front of the roof left or right to align with the header.

The following step by step procedure is necessary to obtain the proper relationship of the roof to the header and rear quarter and the proper timing of lock engagement:

1. Loosen all the mounting screws on the roof lock assemblies just enough to enable the locks to be moved.

2. Push in on the actuating switch until all roof locks stop. Then perform the following steps:

a. Disconnect the right and left flexible drive shafts at the roof motor to remove all drive tension on the roof linkage.

b. Remove the bolts from the base of the roof lift jacks. Loosen the lock nuts and back off the right and left control link adjustment screws until they no longer contact the linkage.

c. Loosen the right and left power link pivot bracket adjustment nuts, four on each side. *Do not relieve the lock washer tension completely or permanent damage will result to the adjusting plate.*

d. On a roof that will not align and lock down, an attempt should be made at this time to lock the roof using a jumper wire at the roof lock power relay. It may be necessary to position the roof manually to align the locks.

3. With the roof securely locked down, check for slack in both roof rear power links. If no slack is apparent, loosen the right and left power link fore-and-aft adjustment screws until slack is evident in both links. Tighten the adjustment screws on each side until the slack is removed. Then tighten an additional ½ turn. Securely tighten the four power link pivot bracket retaining nuts on each side.

4. Screw the control link adjusting screws down until they touch the roof control link. Then tighten the screws an additional two turns (*and no more*). Then tighten the locknuts.

5. Loosen the roof lift jack locknuts and slide the notched washers up and out of the notch in the roof lift jack shafts. Turn the roof lift jack shafts as required to align the roof lift jack bottom bolts. Only one complete turn-adjustment at a time is provided. It may be necessary to turn the flexible drive shafts to obtain alignment of the lower mounting bolts. Install the right and left bolts and position the notched washers. Then tighten the locknuts. Connect and tighten the flexible drive shafts at the roof motor, finger tight.

6. Partially unlock the roof and tighten the front roof locknuts and the rear roof upper and lower lock components. Raise the roof and tighten the roof upper lock components. The upper lock component pivot mounting screw must be tightened first. Then tighten the movable mounting screw.

7. Check the roof lock engagement. The front locks should engage the locknuts slightly before the rear locks. Lock engagement occurs when the lockscrew enters the locknut and should not be confused

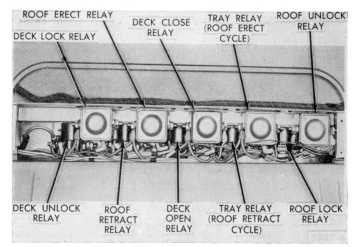

FIG. 180. Identification of relays in control box.

with the rear roof lockscrews entering the rear lockscrew guides. If necessary, the pitch of the roof may be adjusted at the control link adjusting screws. The front of the roof must be blocked at the header to remove the weight of the roof from the roof links while making this adjustment. One turn on the control link adjusting screw will result in approximately $\frac{3}{16}''$ movement at the header.

TROUBLESHOOTING

In the event of trouble, the first step is to check the battery. There must be an adequate supply of power if the top is to operate satisfactorily.

It must be noted that the three roof lock motors are wired in such a way that an open circuit in one motor field winding will cause the current to flow through the other two motors and back to the opposite winding of the motor with the open circuit. This will cause the motor with the open circuit to run in the opposite direction of the other motors, at a reduced speed, and act like a jammed lock.

When a power relay is indicated as an item to check, by-pass the control circuit at that relay as well as checking the relay functionally. Any of the ten basic circuits can be operated by energizing the applicable power relay directly by connecting a jumper wire from the hot terminal of the relay to the relay actuating terminal. This method by-passes all of the various limit switches and operates the motor directly.

However, before by-passing a control circuit, determine audibly

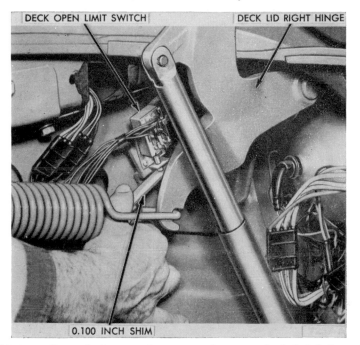

Fig. 181. To adjust deck open limit switch, open deck lid fully. Place a 0.100″ shim between switch plunger and actuator on hinge. Adjust switch firmly against shim with plunger fully depressed. Then tighten switch mounting screws.

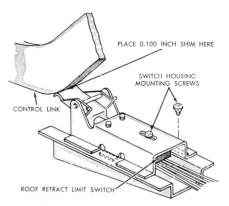

Fig. 182. Roof retract limit switch adjustment. With roof completely retracted and firmly on wheelhouse boots, place a 0.100″ shim between switch actuator and roof control link. Push roof retract limit switch and housing forward firmly to end of its travel. Then tighten switch mounting screws.

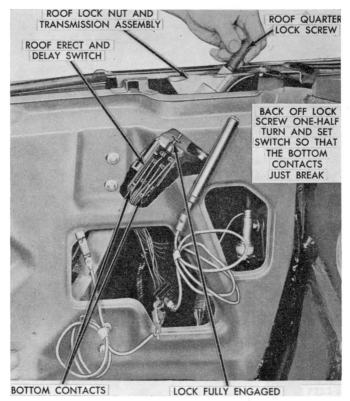

FIG. 183. To make roof erect and delay switch adjustment, secure a new rear roof lock stationary screw; install this lockscrew into rear roof locknut to ratchet point. With a self-powered testlight, connect lead to contacts farthest from switch plunger on roof erect and delay switch. Then back out lockscrew until the light comes on. Switch should be adjusted so that the light comes on at ¾ turn from ratchet point. Roof position "B" switch is adjusted in same manner.

that the motor is not stalled against a jammed lockscrew, or running free due to a broken flexible drive shaft.

If, at any point in the operation, a motor continues to run after a portion of the cycle has been completed, and releasing the actuation switch does not stop the motor, a stuck power relay is indicated. Disconnect the battery before attempting to replace a relay.

If by-passing the control circuit operates the motor, make a continuity check of the components in the particular control circuit involved.

If by-passing the control circuit does not operate the motor, and no mechanical failure is evident, a defective power relay is indicated. The relay may be by-passed by connecting a jumper wire from the hot terminal to the motor feed terminal of the relay. If the relay is not defective, a faulty motor is indicated. Do not overlook the possibility of having a defective circuit breaker, one of which is connected in each motor ground lead.

The following chart lists the possible troubles and the unit causing it. The causes are listed in the order of their probable occurrence.

TROUBLES	CAUSES
1. Deck lid will not unlock on one side	1a. Deck lock flexible drive shaft.
	1b. Deck lock assembly.
2. Deck lid will not unlock on either side	2a. Control wiring circuit breaker.
	2b. Motor feed circuit breaker.
	2c. Neutral switch.
	2d. Actuation switch.
	2e. Deck unlock power relay.
	2f. Deck open limit switch (the contacts closest to the plunger). Roof retract cycle only.
	2g. Roof retract limit switch (contacts farthest from the plunger). Roof erect cycle only.
	2h. Roof erect and delay switch (the contacts second from the plunger). Roof retract cycle only.
	2i. Deck open limit switch (contacts closest to the plunger). Roof erect cycle only.
	2j. Deck lock motor and circuit breaker.
	2k. Deck lock flexible drive shafts.
	2l. Deck lock assemblies.
3. Deck lid unlocks with the cycle indicator light out	3a. Cycle indicator light.
	3b. Deck position "B" switch (the contacts farthest from the plunger together with the deck lock limit switch which energize the cycle indicator light).
	3c. Deck lock limit switch.
4. Deck lid unlocks but will not open	4a. Deck open power relay.
	4b. Deck position "B" switch (the contacts closest to the plunger actuate the deck motor when the deck lid is unlocked.

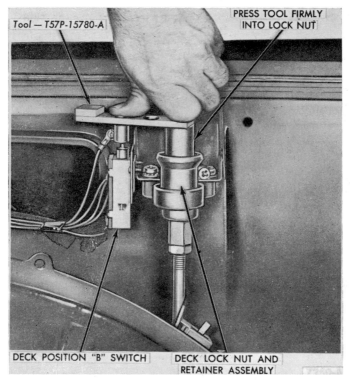

Tool — T57P-15780-A

PRESS TOOL FIRMLY INTO LOCK NUT

DECK POSITION "B" SWITCH

DECK LOCK NUT AND RETAINER ASSEMBLY

FIG. 184. Deck position "B" switch adjustments: (1) To make *actuator* adjustment, position special tool over lockscrew, using the ⅝″ hole in the tool. Then press tool firmly against lockscrew shoulder and pivot tool to line up with deck position "B" switch actuator. Bend actuator until it just touches raised portion of tool. (2) To make *switch* adjustment, operate deck lock limit switch by inserting a small screwdriver between switch plunger and actuator as the cycle light will not go out until both deck lock limit switch and deck position "B" switch are actuated. Press tool firmly into locknut and slide switch upward until cycle indicator light just goes out. Then tighten switch mounting screws.

TROUBLES	CAUSES
	4c. Deck motor and circuit breaker.
	4d. Deck lid flexible drive shafts.
	4e. Deck lid lift jacks.
5. Deck lid opens or closes erratically	5a. Deck lid assist springs.
6. Deck lid opens but the motors will not stop	6a. Deck open limit switch (the contacts closest to the plunger open the circuit to the deck open power relay).
	6b. Deck open power relay.
	6c. Deck unlock power relay.

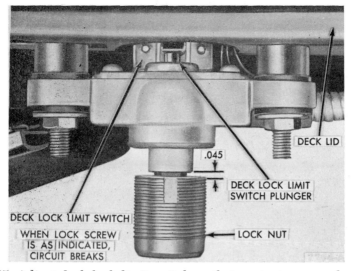

FIG. 185. Adjust deck lock limit switch so that contacts *open* when there is 0.045″ clearance between male and female lock parts. To do this, disconnect deck position "B" switch wires at one connector and screw an extra locknut on the left deck lockscrew to point of ratchet. Then turn ignition switch to ACC position and back off locknut from ratchet point until cycle indicator light comes on. Deck lock limit switch should be adjusted so that the light comes on ½ turn from ratchet point.

TROUBLES	CAUSES
7. Deck lid will not close during the roof retract cycle	7a. Roof retract limit switch (the middle contacts start the deck close cycle).
	7b. Deck position "B" switch (middle contacts).
	7c. Deck motor and circuit breaker.
	7d. Deck lid flexible drive shafts.
	7e. Deck lid lift jacks.
8. Deck lid will not close during the erect cycle	8a. Tray limit switch (the contacts farthest from the plunger start the deck close cycle).
	8b. Deck position "B" switch (middle contacts).
	8c. Deck motor and circuit breaker.
	8d. Deck lid flexible drive shafts.
	8e. Deck lid lift jacks.
	8f. Deck close power relay.
9. Deck lid closes but will not lock	9a. Deck lock motor and circuit breaker.
	9b. Deck lock power relay.
	9c. Deck lock flexible drive shafts.
	9d. Deck lock assemblies.

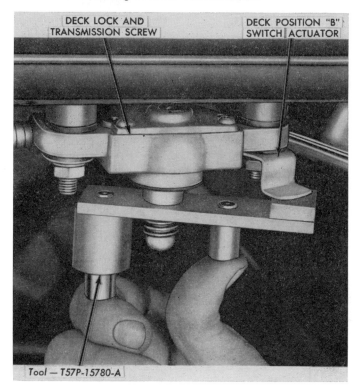

DECK LOCK AND
TRANSMISSION SCREW

DECK POSITION "B"
SWITCH ACTUATOR

Tool — T57P-15780-A

Fig. 186. Deck position "B" switch actuator adjustment. Position tool over lockscrew, using the ⅝" hole in the tool. Then press tool firmly against lockscrew shoulder and pivot tool to line up with deck position "B" switch actuator. Bend actuator with pliers until it just touches raised portion of tool.

TROUBLES	CAUSES
10. Deck lock closes but motor will not stop	10a. Deck position "B" switch (the middle contacts open the circuit to the deck close power relay as the locks engage).
11. Deck lid locks but cycle indicator remains on	11a. Deck position "B" switch (the contacts farthest from the plunger together with the deck lock limit switch energize the cycle indicator lamp).
	11b. Deck lock limit switch.
12. Tray will not extend	12a. Deck open limit switch (the (middle contacts start the tray extend cycle).
	12b. Tray limit switch (the contacts closest to the plunger).

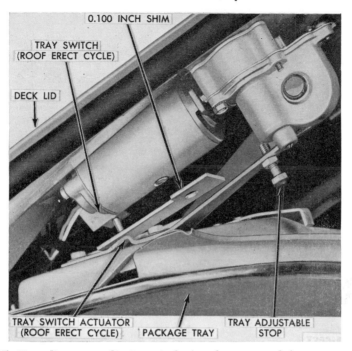

Fig. 187. To adjust tray limit switch (roof erect cycle), actuate power relay so that package tray is folded until motor stalls. Place a 0.100″ shim between end of switch plunger and actuator part of tray support arm. Then push switch to end of its travel against actuator and tighten switch mounting screws.

TROUBLES	CAUSES
	12c. Tray motor and circuit breaker.
	12d. Tray transmission.
	12e. Tray power relay.
13. Tray extends but motor will not stop	13a. Tray limit switch (the contacts closest to the plunger limit the tray extend travel.
	13b. Tray power relay.
14. Tray will not fold	14a. Tray motor and circuit breaker.
	14b. Tray limit switch (the contacts closest to the plunger).
	14c. Tray transmission.
	14d. Tray power relay.
	14e. Roof erect and delay switch (the contacts closest to the plunger start the tray fold cycle).

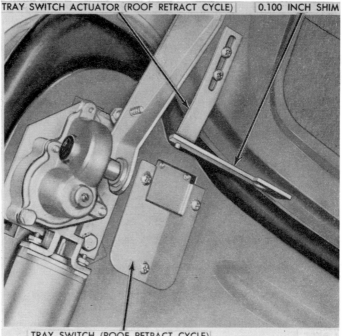

TRAY SWITCH ACTUATOR (ROOF RETRACT CYCLE) | 0.100 INCH SHIM

TRAY SWITCH (ROOF RETRACT CYCLE)

FIG. 188. To adjust tray limit switch (roof retract cycle), actuate power relay so that package tray is extended against tray stops. Then insert a 0.100″ shim between tray switch actuator (roof retract cycle) and end of tray switch plunger. Move actuator toward tray switch (roof retract cycle) until switch plunger is completely depressed. Then tighten actuator attaching screws.

TROUBLES	CAUSES
15. Tray folds but motor will not stop	15a. Tray limit switch (the contacts closest to the plunger limit the tray fold travel).
	15b. Tray power relay.
16. Left rear roof lock will not operate	16a. Left roof lock motor and circuit breaker.
	16b. Roof lock flexible drive shaft.
	16c. Roof lock assembly.
17. Right rear roof lock will not operate	17a. Right roof lock motor and circuit breaker.
	17b. Roof lock flexible drive shaft.
	17c. Roof lock assembly.
18. Front roof locks will not operate	18a. Front roof lock motor and circuit breaker.
	18b. Front roof lock flexible drive shafts.
	18c. Front roof lock assemblies.

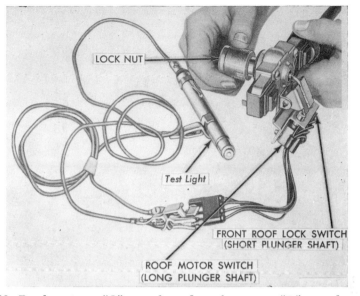

LOCK NUT

Test Light

FRONT ROOF LOCK SWITCH
(SHORT PLUNGER SHAFT)

ROOF MOTOR SWITCH
(LONG PLUNGER SHAFT)

FIG. 189. Roof position "C" switch and roof position "D" switch are adjusted with lockscrew and switch assemblies removed from car. The two switches are arranged side-by-side and function to control two circuits simultaneously; one controls the front roof lock circuit and the other the roof motor circuit.

To adjust front roof lock circuit switch (short plunger shaft), screw a spare locknut fully onto lockscrew to the point of ratchet. Attach a self-powered test light to switch circuit and back off locknut until test light goes on. The light should go on at ¾ turn from ratchet point.

Roof motor switch (long plunger shaft) should light the light one full turn before lockscrew threads disengage.

TROUBLES	CAUSES
19. Roof will not unlock—all locks	19a. Tray limit switch (the contacts farthest from the plunger start the roof unlock cycle).
	19b. Roof position "B" switch (contacts with the yellow wires).
	19c. Roof unlock power relay.
20. Roof unlocks but will not retract	20a. Roof motor and circuit breaker.
	20b. Roof retract limit switch (the contacts closest to the plunger).
	20c. Roof flexible drive shafts.
	20d. Roof lift jacks.
	20e. Roof retract power relay.
	20f. Roof position "D" switch (the switch with the long plunger).

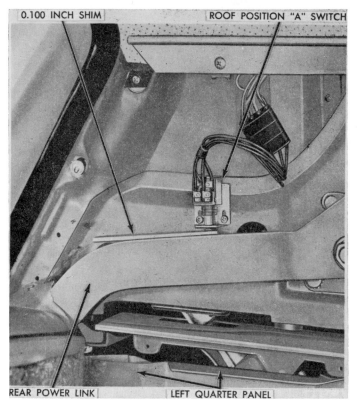

0.100 INCH SHIM | ROOF POSITION "A" SWITCH

REAR POWER LINK | LEFT QUARTER PANEL

FIG. 190. Roof position "A" switch adjustment is made with roof erected and in the fully locked down position. Adjust switch against roof rear power link with a 0.100″ shim between switch plunger and roof link. Slide switch firmly against power link to end of plunger travel, and then tighten switch mounting screws.

TROUBLES	CAUSES
	20g. Roof position "C" switch (the switch with the long plunger).
	20h. Roof position "B" switch (the contacts closest to the plunger).
	20i. Roof erect and delay switch (the second set of contacts from the plunger).
21. Front roof panel will not fold or unfold	21a. Front roof power linkage.
22. Roof will not erect	22a. Deck open limit switch (the contacts farthest from the plunger start the roof erect cycle).

TROUBLES

CAUSES

22b. Roof erect power relay.

22c. Roof position "B" switch (the middle contacts).

22d. Roof motor and circuit breaker.

23. Roof erects but will not lock—all locks

23a. Roof position "A" switch (the contacts with the red and green wires attached start the lock cycle).

23b. Roof lock power relay.

24. Roof motor will not stop during the roof retract cycle

24a. Roof retract limit switch (the contacts closest to the plunger limit the roof retract travel).

24b. Roof retract power relay.

25. Roof motor will not stop during the roof erect cycle

25a. Roof erect power relay.

25b. Roof position "B" switch (the middle contacts stop the roof motor when the locks engage).

26. Roof lock motors will not stop

26a. Roof lock power relay (if motor will not stop when actuation switch is released).

26b. Roof position "B" switch (the contacts farthest from the plunger).

26c. Roof erect and delay switch (the third set of contacts from the plunger).

26d. Roof position "C" switch (the switch with the short plunger).

26e. Roof position "D" switch (the switch with the short plunger).

26f. Roof and roof lock alignment.

CONVERTIBLE POWER TOPS

OPERATION

The convertible top is raised and lowered by two hydraulic cylinders which are actuated by oil pressure received from a rotor-type pump driven by an electric motor. The motor, pump, and oil reservoir form a compact unit located under the rear seat cushion. One hydraulic cylinder is located behind each quarter trim panel. Each hydraulic cylinder is connected to the pump by two lines. Oil flows through these lines in either direction determined by whether the top is being raised or lowered.

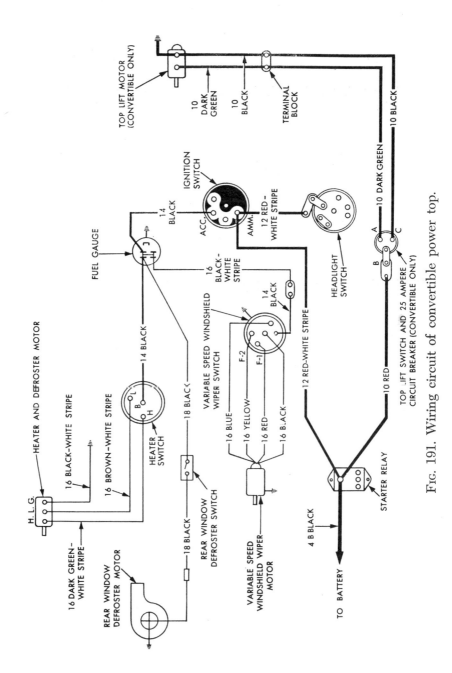

FIG. 191. Wiring circuit of convertible power top.

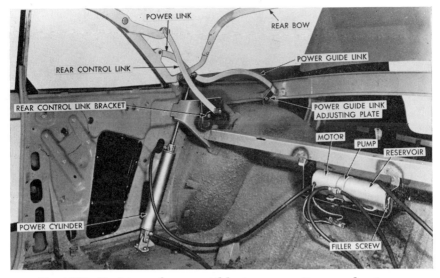

Fig. 192. Position of convertible top operating mechanisms.

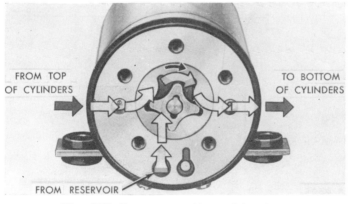

Fig. 193. Pump operation raising top.

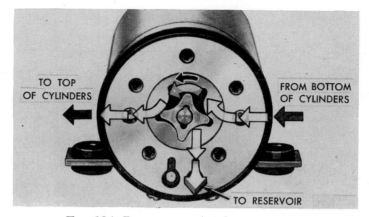

FIG. 194. Pump operation lowering top.

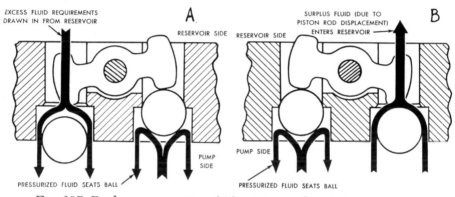

FIG. 195. Rocker arm position (A) raising and (B) lowering top.

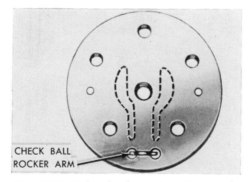

FIG. 196. Valve body and rocker arm.

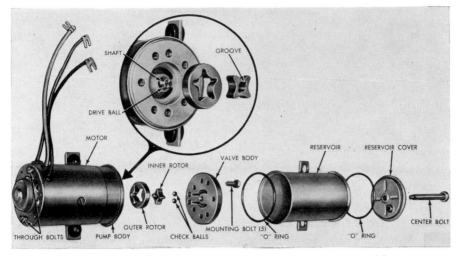

FIG. 197. Exploded view of motor and pump assembly.

When the top-control button on the instrument panel is pushed *forward,* battery voltage is supplied to the motor through the yellow wire. The motor and pump assembly then operates to force fluid through the hoses to the lower ends of the hydraulic cylinders. The fluid forces the piston rods up, and the top is raised. The fluid in the top of the cylinders returns to the pump and is recirculated to the bottom of the cylinders.

When the top-control button is pulled *rearward,* battery voltage is supplied to the motor through the red wire. The motor and pump assembly now operates in a reversed direction to force fluid through the hoses to the top of the hydraulic cylinders. The fluid forces the piston rods down, and the top is lowered. The fluid in the bottom of the cylinders returns to the pump and is recirculated to the top of the cylinders.

SERVICE PROCEDURES

Motor and Pump Assembly:

Removal:
   1. Operate the top to the full *up* position.
   2. Disconnect the positive battery cable.
   3. Remove the rear seat cushion.
   4. Disconnect the motor leads at the junction block, and disconnect the ground wire.

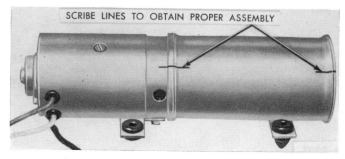

Fɪɢ. 198. A scribed line assists in assembly.

5. Remove the attaching screws, and remove the motor and pump assembly from the floor pan. Do not misplace the rubber grommets.

6. Vent the reservoir by removing the filler plug, and then reinstall the filler plug. The reservoir must be vented to equalize the pressure to lessen the possibility of fluid spraying on the trim and paint when the hoses are disconnected.

7. Place absorbent cloths beneath the hose connections, disconnect the hoses, and then plug the open fittings and lines to prevent the entrance of dirt.

Disassembly:

1. Remove the filler plug and drain the fluid from the reservoir into a clean container.

2. Scribe lines on the reservoir, pump body, and reservoir cover for correct reassembly.

3. Remove the center bolt from the reservoir cover.

4. Remove the cover and reservoir and the two "O" ring seals at each end of the reservoir.

5. Remove the mounting bolts retaining the valve body to the pump body.

6. Place a cloth under the assembly, and then carefully remove the valve body so that the check balls are not lost.

7. Remove the inner and outer rotor and the drive ball.

Assembly. Use all parts contained in the pump repair kit. If the reservoir or seals indicate the need, use the reservoir repair kit also.

1. Install the drive ball and the inner rotor on the armature shaft.

2. Install the outer rotor over the inner rotor.

3. Place the check balls in the pump body channels.

4. Install the valve body on the pump body.

5. Install the valve body mounting bolts.

6. Install an "O" ring seal in each end of the reservoir.

7. Install a new seal on the center bolt, and then install the reservoir and cover on the valve body using the lines previously scribed as guides. Be sure that the stamped ribs in the cover are straight, both vertically and horizontally. The filler plug must be in the upper left-hand corner.

8. Place the assembly in a horizontal position, fill the reservoir with brake fluid to the level of the bottom of the filler plug hole, and then install the filler plug with a new seal.

Installation:

1. Remove the plugs from the lines and fittings. Connect the lines to the pump. Use cloths to absorb any fluid which leaks out of the lines or pump.

2. Install the assembly on the floor pan, making sure that the rubber grommets are in their proper places under the mounting brackets.

3. Connect the motor lead wires at the junction block, and then connect the ground wire.

4. Connect the battery positive cable.

5. Operate the top assembly two or three times to bleed air from the system. With the top in its full *up* position, refill the reservoir with fluid.

6. Install the rear seat cushion.

Lift Cylinder:

Removal:

1. Disconnect the battery positive cable.

2. Remove the rear seat cushion and the cushion back.

3. Remove the quarter trim panel.

4. Disconnect and plug the hydraulic lines at the upper and lower ends of the cylinder. Use absorbent cloths to catch any leaking fluid.

5. Remove the hair pin clip and clevis pin at each end of the cylinder. Then remove the cylinder.

Installation:

1. Position the new cylinder in the floor bracket with the hose connections facing down.

2. Install the clevis pins and hair pin clips at each end of the cylinder.

3. Connect the hydraulic lines to the cylinder.

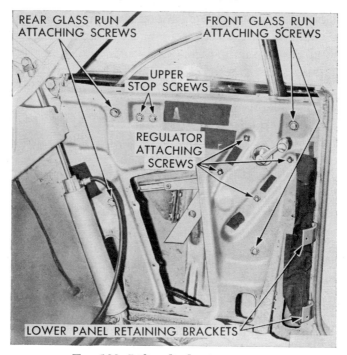

REAR GLASS RUN ATTACHING SCREWS

FRONT GLASS RUN ATTACHING SCREWS

UPPER STOP SCREWS

REGULATOR ATTACHING SCREWS

LOWER PANEL RETAINING BRACKETS

FIG. 199. Lift cylinder in position.

4. Connect the battery positive cable.

5. Operate the top assembly two or three times to bleed air from the system.

6. Check the reservoir fluid level.

7. Install the quarter trim panel, the rear seat back, and the cushion.

TROUBLESHOOTING

TROUBLES	CAUSES
1. Top action too slow	1a. Binding in the linkage.
	1b. Battery voltage too low.
	1c. Poor connections.
	1d. Kinked hoses.
	1e. Defective pump.
2. One piston moves faster than the other	2a. The cylinder with the slow moving piston rod is defective.
3. Top does not move at all	3a. Defective pump.
	3b. Defective top control switch.
	3c. Defective circuit breaker.
	3d. Insufficient fluid.

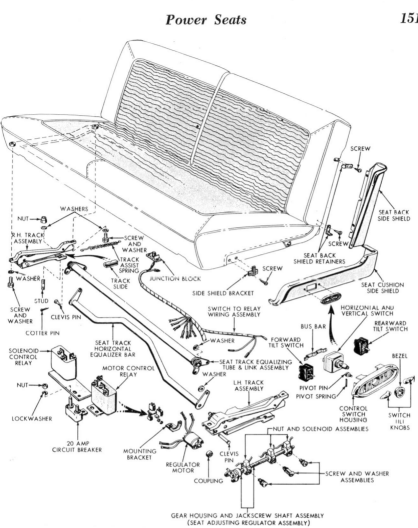

FIG. 200. Six-way power seat.

POWER SEATS

Power seats are designed to move in up to six directions; back and forth, up and down, and a tilt movement. In one design (Seat-O-Matic), a built-in switching device returns the seat to a previously selected set of conditions when the ignition switch is turned *on*.

Six-Way Power Seat. The six-way power seat contains the usual horizontal and vertical seat movements and, in addition, provides a forward tilt adjustment whereby the forward end of the seat assembly may be tilted or inclined upward or downward and a rear

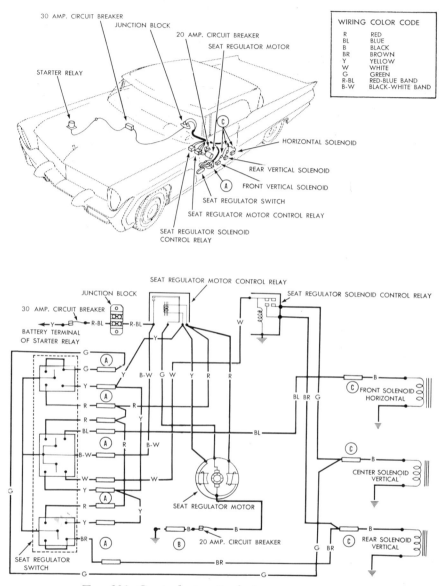

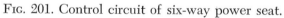

Fig. 201. Control circuit of six-way power seat.

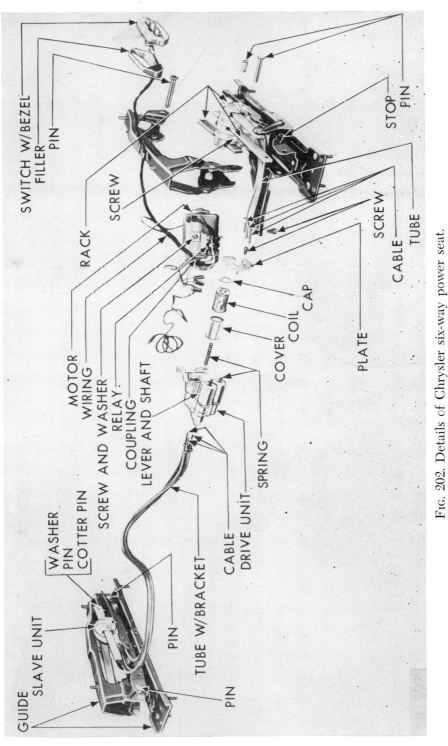

GUIDE
SLAVE UNIT
PIN
TUBE W/BRACKET
PIN

WASHER
PIN
COTTER PIN
SCREW AND WASHER
RELAY
COUPLING
LEVER AND SHAFT
CABLE
DRIVE UNIT
SPRING

MOTOR
WIRING

COVER
COIL
CAP

PLATE

RACK
SCREW

SWITCH W/BEZEL
FILLER
PIN

STOP
PIN

SCREW
CABLE
TUBE

Fig. 202. Details of Chrysler six-way power seat.

153

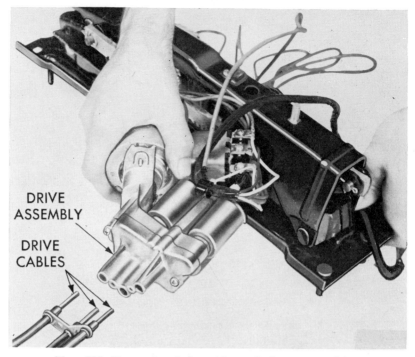

FIG. 203. Removing left guide and drive assembly.

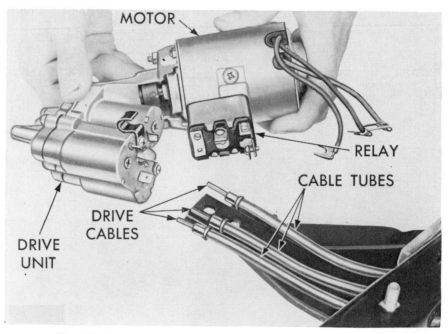

FIG. 204. Removing drive assembly from left slave unit.

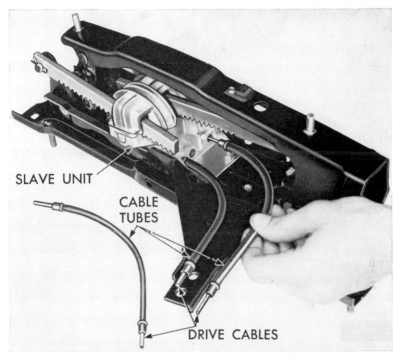

Fig. 205. Installing cable tubes in slave unit.

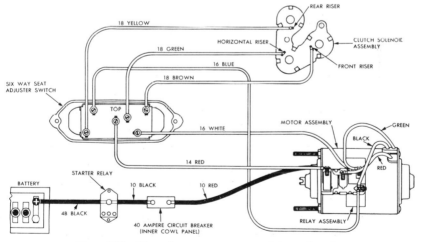

Fig. 206. Chrysler power seat wiring circuit.

tilt adjustment through which the rearward end of the seat assembly may be tilted upward or downward.

The seat adjustments are controlled by a cluster of three switch assemblies located on the left side seat shield. The center switch in the cluster is a four-way switch which controls the horizontal and vertical adjustments. A two-way switch, located forward of the center switch, controls the forward tilt adjustment, and another two-way switch, located at the rear of the cluster, controls the rearward tilt adjustment.

The seat adjuster actuator mechanism, located under the left side of the seat assembly, consists of a reversible electric motor, regulator motor control relay, a 20 ampere circuit breaker, a regulator solenoid control relay, a gear housing and jackscrew shaft assembly (seat adjusting regulator assembly), and three spinning nut and solenoid assemblies which are meshed to the jackscrew shaft. The spinning nut and solenoid assemblies are individually connected through bellcranks, the track equalizing tube and link assembly, and the horizontal track equalizing bar, to the right and left seat track assemblies.

The gear housing and jackscrew shaft assembly consists of a driving worm gear and a driven gear which rotates the jackscrew shaft. The driving worm gear is connected to the motor by a coupling, therefore, when the motor is energized, the driven gear rotates the jackscrew shaft.

The three spinning nut and solenoid assemblies are identical in construction. Each one consists of an internally threaded sector or nut coupled with a locking solenoid. The principle of operation of the nut and solenoid assembly is comparable to the threading action of a bolt rotating through a stationary nut. As each solenoid is energized, the internally threaded nut is locked stationary by the solenoid pawl engaging a notch on the nut. As the jackscrew shaft is rotated through the locked internal nut, the nut and solenoid assembly is caused to move along the shaft. This threading movement adjusts, through the bellcrank to an equalizer bar, the left and right seat track assemblies to locate the seat in the desired position.

A number of roll pins, inserted through the diameter of the jackscrew shaft, limit the shaft and nut threading action when the seat reaches its extreme positions. The length of the roll pins is greater than the jackscrew shaft diameter, so that the nut contacts the protruding ends of a roll pin as the seat reaches its extreme position. As the nut butts against the revolving roll pin, the pin slips into

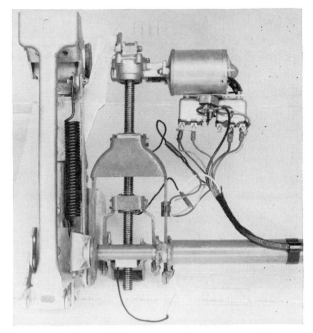

Fig. 207. Closeup of threaded screw and operating linkages of Mercury power seat.

Fig. 208. Jackscrew and shaft assembly with spinning nut and solenoid assemblies.

notches in the end of the nut, thereby locking the nut to the revolving jackscrew shaft. This locking action disengages the solenoid pawl from the nut and it rotates with the jackscrew shaft and freewheels in its solenoid housing.

The various seat motions are controlled by the three nut and solenoid assemblies as follows:

> Horizontal (fore and aft)—front nut
> Vertical (up and down)—center and rear nuts
> Rear tilt—rear nut
> Front tilt—front nut

The nut and solenoid assemblies which do not function in adjusting the seat are not energized and utilize the free-wheeling feature by rotating with the jackscrew.

TROUBLESHOOTING

TROUBLES	CAUSES
1. Seat motor does not operate in any switch position	1a. Broken wire or loose connection.
	1b. Defective 30 amp circuit breaker located behind the glove compartment.
	1c. Defective 20 amp circuit breaker located on front pan at left front edge of front seat assembly.
	1d. Seat control switch inoperative.
	1e. Seat regulator motor control relay inoperative.
	1f. Seat motor inoperative.
	1g. Driven gear and jackscrew shaft and/or nut assemblies bound up.
2. Seat motor operates in some switch positions, but does not operate in all positions	2a. Broken wire or loose connection in the switch control circuit from the affected switch.
	2b. Seat control switch inoperative.
3. Seat motor operates but the jackscrew shaft does not rotate	3a. Coupling between motor and driving worm gear worn or broken.
	3b. Seat regulator driving worm and driven gears worn, broken, or loose on jackscrew shaft.
4. Jackscrew shaft rotates but the seat does not move	4a. Broken wire or loose connection between the seat control switch and the inoperative

TROUBLES CAUSES

jackscrew shaft nut and solenoid assembly.

4b. Open circuit in seat control
switch.

4c. Jackscrew shaft nut and solenoid assembly malfunction.

Solenoid: Check the continuity of current through the
solenoid coil on the nut assembly. The ground wire must
be securely grounded on the
nut.

Nut: Disassemble the regulator nut assembly and check
for correctness of assembly and
for sticking, binding, or broken
internal parts.

Fig. 209. Dash control unit of Seat-O-Matic power seat.

Seat-O-Matic Power Seat. The Seat-O-Matic power seat is a two-
motor, four-way power seat with an electrical control system to
place the seat automatically in any one of five pre-selected vertical
positions or seven horizontal positions. The seat will automatically

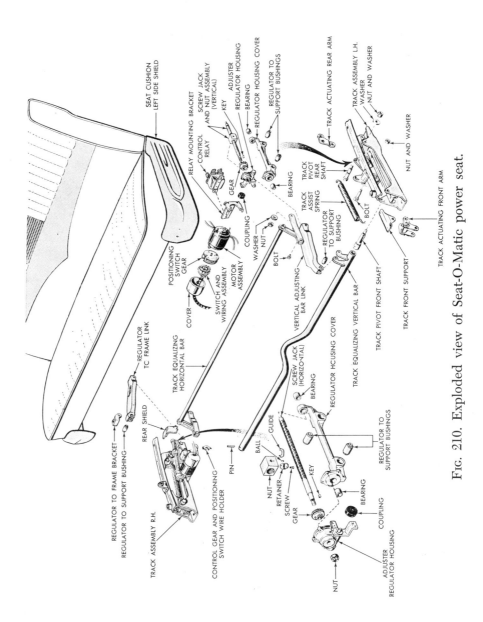

FIG. 210. Exploded view of Seat-O-Matic power seat.

be moved to the extreme rear position whenever the ignition key is turned to the *off* position and will be moved to one of the seven pre-selected horizontal positions, indicated on the dial control, whenever the key is again turned to the *ON* or *ACC* position.

Parts. The *easy entry seat relay* is located on the left front fender apron. It allows the seat to return to the extreme rear position by completing the circuit to the No. 7 terminal of the *horizontal motor seat positioning switch* when the ignition key is turned to the *OFF* position. When the ignition key is turned to the *ON* or *ACC* position, the relay completes the circuit to the seat horizontal positioning switch which then assumes control and moves the seat to the pre-selected position. The *seat dial control switch* on the instrument panel is a combination of two multiple contact switches. The horizontal switch incorporates seven contacts and is controlled by the outer bezel. The No. 1 position places the seat farthest forward. The other contacts place the seat in corresponding positions toward the rear. The vertical switch has five contacts and is controlled by the center knob. The *A* position places the seat in the highest position. The other four positions place the seat in corresponding downward positions.

The *horizontal and vertical motor seat positioning switches* are mounted under the seat on the rear of their respective motors and are driven through clock-like gear reduction mechanisms. The wafer switches establish the position of the seat by interrupting the seat regulator control relay circuits when the seat reaches a pre-selected position.

The *seat regulator control relay* completes the seat regulator motor armature and field circuits as dictated by the seat dial control and motor positioning switches.

Theory of Operation. The circuit operation of only the vertical adjustment is described because the horizontal motor control is similar.

The motor positioning wafer switch consists of an upper switch plate (indicated by solid lines) and a lower switch plate (indicated by dash lines). The upper plate may contact the *A, B, C,* and *D* terminals. The lower plate may contact the *B, C, D,* and *E* terminals. The yellow wire to the vertical seat regulator control relay contacts only the lower switch plate. The red wire to the control relay contacts only the upper switch plate.

The seat dial control is set for the *C* position in the circuit drawing (Fig. 211), and the seat is stopped in the middle vertical posi-

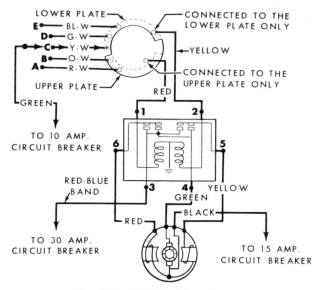

FIG. 211. "C" position circuit.

tion. The C terminal of the wafer switch is not in contact with either the upper or the lower plates of the motor wafer switch and both circuits to the control relay windings are open.

With the seat still in the C (middle) position, the seat dial control has now been placed in the A position (Fig. 212). Current now flows from the A terminal of the seat dial control switch to the A terminal of the motor wafer switch, which is in contact with only the upper plate. From the upper plate, current flows through the red wire to the seat regulator control relay winding which closes the relay points and energizes the circuit from the circuit breaker to the motor armature and field. The motor then drives the seat and rotates the switch plates until the plates reach the position shown in Fig. 213. When this position is reached, the circuit to the seat regulator control relay winding is broken, and the relay points *open,* stopping the motor at the selected A position.

In Fig. 214 the seat is in the A position and the seat dial control is in the B position. The seat must now be made to move in the opposite direction. Current flows from the B terminal of the seat dial control switch to the B terminal of the motor wafer switch. The B terminal is in contact with the lower plate only. Current flows from the lower plate through the yellow wire to the other winding of the seat regulator control relay. The relay points are thus closed, and the motor armature and field circuits are completed. The seat

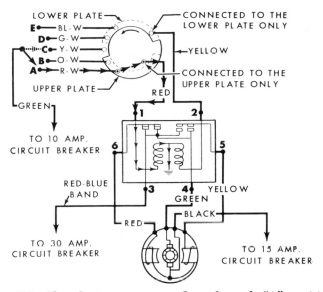

Fig. 212. Closed circuit current flow through "A" position.

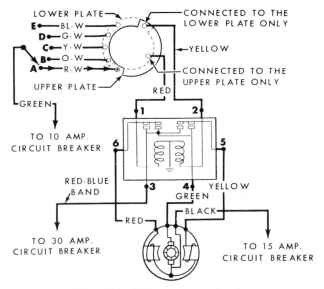

Fig. 213. "A" position circuit.

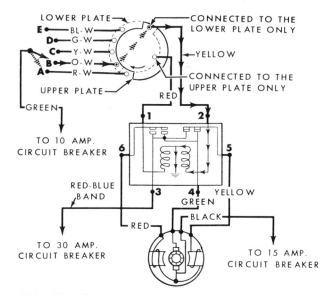

FIG. 214. Closed circuit current flow through "B" position.

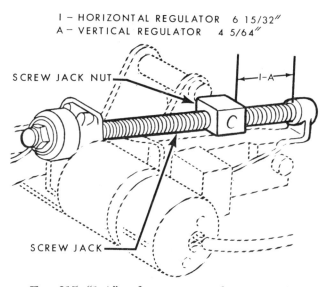

FIG. 215. "1-A" index position of screw jack.

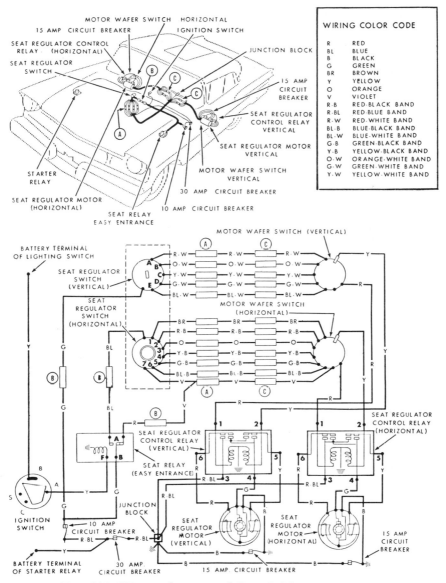

Fig. 216. Wiring diagram of Seat-O-Matic power seat.

regulator motor rotates in the opposite direction until the motor wafer switch is in a position where the lower plate is no longer in contact with either *B* terminal. The relay winding is no longer energized and the relay contacts open.

Service Procedures. In the event either of the regulator motors are to be removed, the seat should be placed in the "*1-A*" position be-

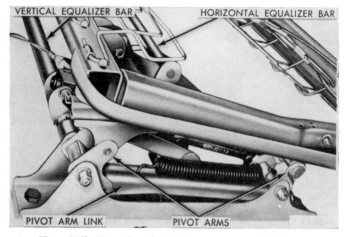

VERTICAL EQUALIZER BAR   HORIZONTAL EQUALIZER BAR

PIVOT ARM LINK   PIVOT ARMS

Fig. 217. Details of Ford power seat linkage.

fore any disassembly work is started. This position is obtained by locating the "*1-A*" index position of the jackscrew (Fig. 215).

Troubleshooting. The complete system should be carefully examined for loose connections, burned or chafed wires, and open circuits. The seat regulator should also be inspected to be sure it is functioning correctly. **CAUTION:** *Should it be necessary to operate the seat regulator motors independently of the seat dial control, extreme caution should be exercised to prevent extending the seat past normal extreme positions;* otherwise, the seat track and associated parts will be damaged.

Troubleshooting Chart

TROUBLES	CAUSES
1. Seat will not move vertically or horizontally when the seat dial control switch positions are changed	1a. Defective 10 or 30 ampere circuit breaker.
2. Seat will not move up or down but will move fore or aft	2a. Defective seat vertical regulator motor or control relay.
3. Seat will not move fore or aft but will move up or down	3a. Defective easy entry seat relay or horizontal seat regulator motor or relay.
4. Seat control is erratic and skips some positions	4a. Damaged (open) contacts on the seat control and/or motor wafer switch or poor connections in the wiring harness.

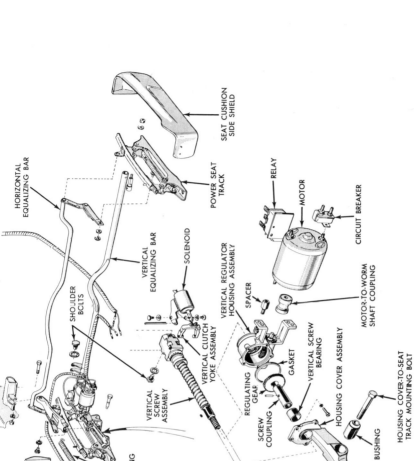

SEAT CUSHION SIDE SHIELD

HORIZONTAL EQUALIZING BAR

POWER SEAT TRACK

VERTICAL EQUALIZING BAR

RELAY

MOTOR

CIRCUIT BREAKER

SOLENOID

SHOULDER BOLTS

VERTICAL REGULATOR HOUSING ASSEMBLY

SPACER

MOTOR-TO-WORM SHAFT COUPLING

VERTICAL CLUTCH YOKE ASSEMBLY

VERTICAL SCREW ASSEMBLY

REGULATING GEAR

GASKET

VERTICAL SCREW BEARING

HOUSING COVER ASSEMBLY

SCREW COUPLING

HOUSING COVER-TO-SEAT TRACK MOUNTING BOLT

BUSHING

ASSIST SPRING

4-WAY SWITCH

HORIZONTAL SCREW ASSEMBLY

SOLENOID

HORIZONTAL CLUTCH YOKE ASSEMBLY

HORIZONTAL SCREW BEARING

Fig. 218. Exploded view of Ford seat parts.

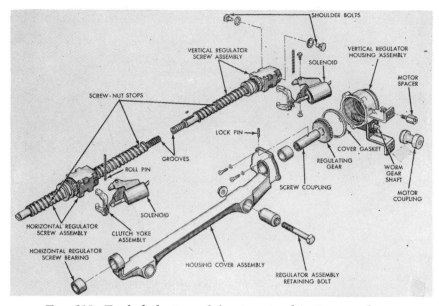

FIG. 219. Exploded view of front seat adjusting regulator.

Four-Way Power Seat. The four-way power seat is controlled by a single toggle switch which can be operated in four directions. Moving the seat switch *up* or *down* and *fore* or *aft* causes the seat to move in the direction in which the seat switch is moved. The switch is mounted on the instrument panel.

Power is provided by a single electric motor which drives a screw jack. A magnetic clutch (solenoid) is located at each end of the screw jack. When the switch is operated for *up* or *down* seat motion, the front magnetic clutch engages the screw jack, and the seat is raised or lowered by two pivot arms at each side of the seat. The *up* or *down* motion is transmitted to the right seat track by a vertical equalizer bar.

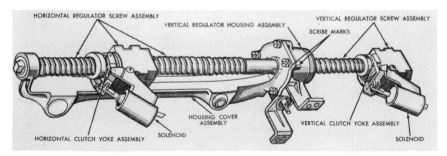

FIG. 220. Details of assembly of front seat adjusting regulator.

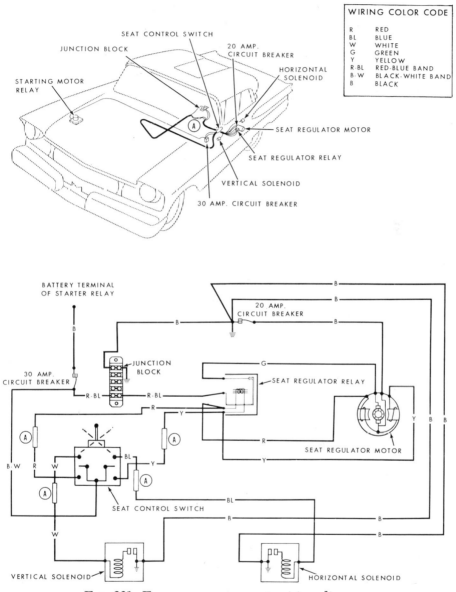

Fig. 221. Four-way power seat wiring diagram.

When the seat switch is operated for *fore* or *aft* movement, the rear magnetic clutch engages the screw jack, and the seat is moved *forward* or *rearward* by the horizontal movement arm. The *fore* and *aft* motion is transmitted to the right seat track by a horizontal equalizer bar.

TROUBLESHOOTING CHART

TROUBLES	CAUSES
1. Seat will not operate in any direction	1a. Short circuit or defective motor.
2. Seat moves *fore* and *aft* or *up* and *down* only	2a. Defective magnetic clutch (solenoid) or its wiring.
3. Seat moves opposite to switch	3a. Crossed wires at the switch or relay.
4. Seat operates sluggishly	4a. Binding in the seat track or screw jack.
	4b. Defective motor.

ELECTRICALLY OPERATED WINDOW

Operation. When the ignition switch is turned to the *ON* or *ACC* position, current from the ignition switch flows to and through the window safety relay to ground. The energizing of the relay closes the relay points, causing battery current to flow to the control switch cluster and individually located switches. Actuation of the cluster closes the circuit to the respective window motor armature and field winding.

Service Procedures:

Removal of Front Door Window Electric Motor and/or Regulator Assembly:

1. Lower the window assembly to its full *down* position.
2. Disconnect the battery ground cable to prevent shorts.
3. Remove the arm rest support from the door inner panel.
4. Peel the plastic shield down to the lower edge of the door.
5. To remove the motor only, disconnect the motor wires at the bullet connectors. Remove the two nuts and eyelets securing the motor assembly and coupling to the regulator assembly. Remove the motor and coupling through the door inner panel access hole.

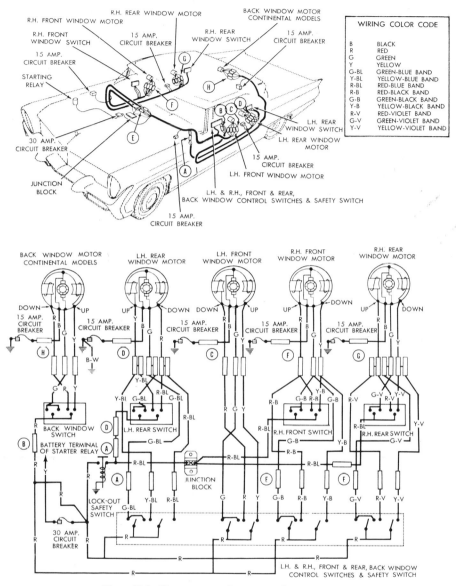

FIG. 222. Power window regulator circuit.

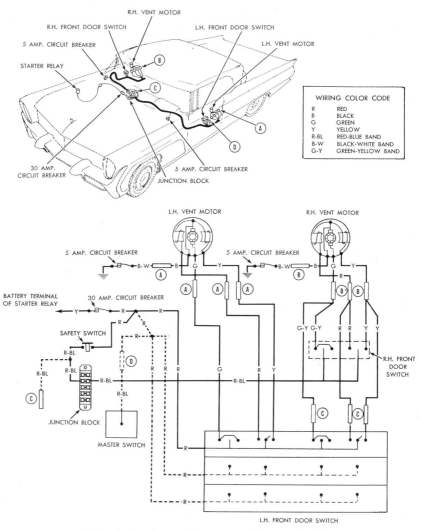

FIG. 223. Vent window regulator circuit.

6. To remove the regulator and motor as an assembly, remove the cap screws securing the window lower stop to the door inner panel. Remove the stop. Disconnect the motor wires at the bullet connectors. With the window lowered to the full *down* position, remove the two spring-type retainers that secure the window channel roller assemblies to the window regulator arms. Separate the regulator arm pivots from the rollers. Raise the window assembly to the full *up* position and retain the window with a rubber wedge.

Remove the cap screws holding the regulator assembly to the door inner panel and remove the regulator and motor as an assembly.

Installation of Front Door Window Electric Motor and/or Regulator Assembly:

1. To install the motor only, secure the motor and coupling to the regulator with two steel eyelets and nuts. To obtain proper torque, tighten the nuts until the two eyelets on each side of the rubber grommet, in the motor mounting flange, butt together. Connect the motor wires.

2. To install the regulator and motor assembly, assemble the cup washers, springs, and flat washers onto the rollers. Install it on the window channel roller guides and secure it with spring-type retainers. Lubricate the roller assemblies, window channel guides, and center pivot and quadrant of the regulator assembly with Lubriplate. Install the regulator and motor as an assembly into the door and secure it to the door inner panel with cap screws. Connect the motor wires at the bullet connectors. Remove the rubber wedge and lower the window assembly until the rollers are in line with the pivots on the regulator arms. Press the regulator arm pivots into the roller assemblies until the retainers drop into the pivot grooves. Tempo-

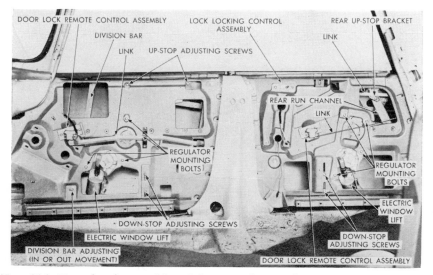

Fig. 224. Details of assembly of front and rear door power window lift mechanisms.

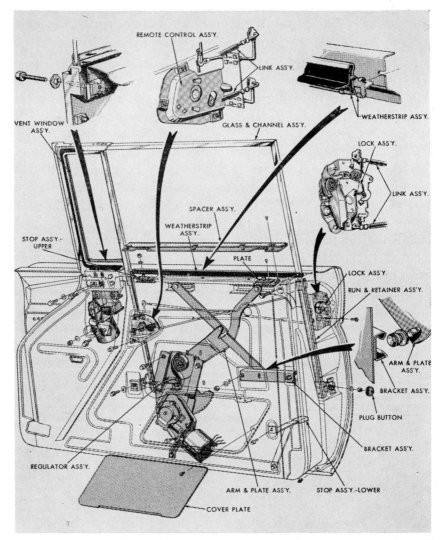

FIG. 225. Details of assembly of Lincoln front door power window lift and vent window operating mechanisms.

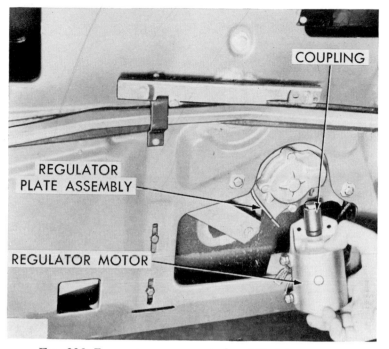

Fɪɢ. 226. Removing power window lift drive motor.

rarily connect the battery ground cable and check the assembly for proper operation. Complete the installation of the remaining parts by reversing the order of removal.

TROUBLESHOOTING

TROUBLES	CAUSES
1. One window operates in one direction only through either switch circuit	1a. One winding in motor open or shorted.
2. Window operates in both directions through one switch circuit only	2a. Defective switch.
3. One window will not operate in either direction through either switch circuit	3a. Motor armature and/or windings open or shorted. 3b. 15 ampere (motor ground) circuit breaker improperly grounded or defective.
4. All windows will not operate in either direction	4a. Safety relay or 30 ampere circuit breaker defective.

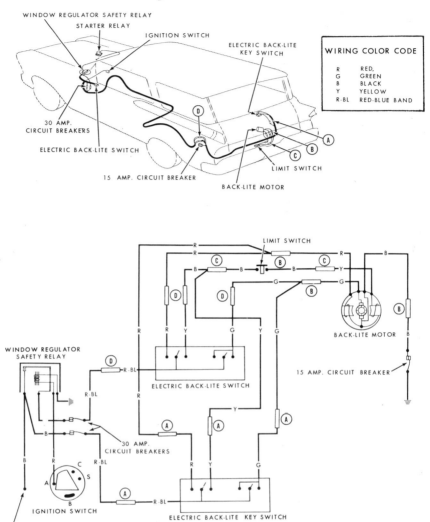

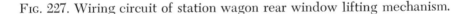

Fɪɢ. 227. Wiring circuit of station wagon rear window lifting mechanism.

REVIEW QUESTIONS

1. What type of power is used to operate the Ford retractable hardtop?
2. What is the purpose of the gearshift interlock switch?
3. In what way can the roof motion be reversed?
4. What must occur, during the roof retract cycle, before the deck lid can be opened?
5. What actuates the roof position "D" switch?
6. What is the first part to move in the roof erect cycle?
7. When is a roof adjustment necessary?
8. What are the three basic adjustments?

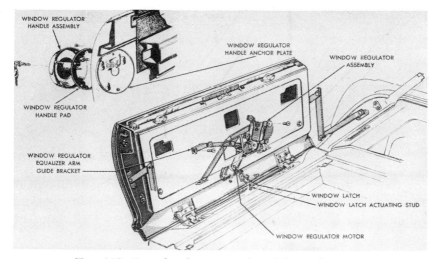

FIG. 228. Details of rear window lift mechanism.

9. What is the first troubleshooting step suggested?
10. How can you tell that a motor has an open field winding?
11. How many basic circuits are there?
12. How can you by-pass a suspected relay?
13. What type of power is used to operate the convertible power top?
14. In how many directions are power seats designed to operate?
15. What type of power is used to operate power seats?
16. What special characteristic belongs to the Seat-O-Matic power seat unit?
17. When servicing the Seat-O-Matic unit, what precaution is given in regard to positioning the seat before any disassembly work is to begin?
18. What is the function of the safety relay in the electrically operated window system?

5

TEMPERATURE CONTROL
DEVICES

As the comfort of the driver and passengers is of paramount importance in the engineering of the modern automobile, optional equipment has been designed to heat the car's interior in winter and to cool it in summer.

Hot-water type heaters have been in common use for many years. They circulate the engine coolant through a small radiator core located within the passenger compartment. An electric motor drives a fan which blows air through the core to heat it.

Hot-water type heaters, using the engine coolant, are less effective when the outside temperature is at a minimum—a time when heater demand is at a maximum. Then, too, the engine runs cooler when the outside air temperature is lower unless a special higher-opening, heater-type thermostat is installed in the engine cooling system. Another defect of hot water heaters is that they do not deliver heat until the engine is warmed up.

To overcome these defects, a gasoline-burning unit has been developed as optional equipment by some manufacturers. Gasoline is drawn from the car's fuel system, sprayed into a combustion chamber, and ignited by a constantly firing spark plug. Heat is delivered to the passenger compartment in about one minute of operation.

An air conditioner, a recent development offered as optional equipment, cools the interior of the car through the principle of refrigeration. It contains provisions for dehumidifying the air and cleaning it of dust and dirt. As an air reheating device is required in an air conditioning system, the usual hot water heater is incorporated. In winter, the heater section is used alone to warm the interior of the car. Thus the air conditioning system works the year-'round for the comfort of the motorist.

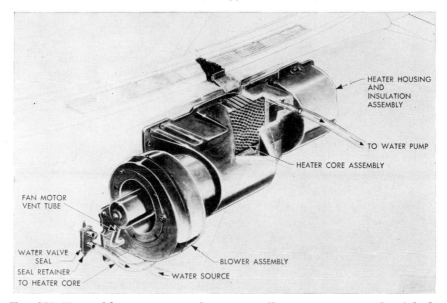

FIG. 229. Typical hot-water type heater installation on engine side of dash.

HOT-WATER TYPE HEATERS

Fresh air enters through an air intake grille where a blower forces it through the heater core. Heated air is then distributed across the front compartment floor. A damper, inside the plenum chamber, directs air to the windshield defroster outlets when the heater control is at the *DEF* position and to the floor when the control is at the *HEATER* position. A thermostat adjusts the water control valve regulating the water temperature in the heater core.

Most control systems contain provisions for the driver to allow more or less outside air to pass through the heater. The more complex systems use automatic controls to position the vents. Generally, a two- or three-position heater blower switch is provided.

GASOLINE-BURNING TYPE HEATERS

Operation. The heater is a combustion type, gasoline-burning unit. When the heater blower switch is turned on, the following events occur simultaneously:

The fuel valve coil is energized and operates the valve permitting fuel to flow to the heater. The burner blower and the fuel pump motor start. The electrical circuit is completed to the ignition unit which causes a continuous vibrating spark to occur in the spark plug electrode gap, igniting the fuel mixture. The ventilator air blower

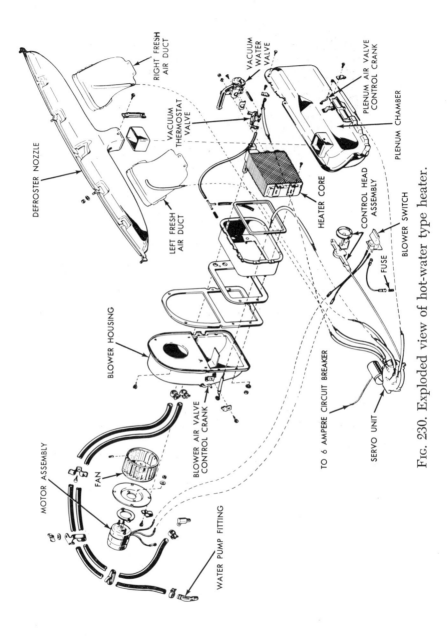

FIG. 230. Exploded view of hot-water type heater.

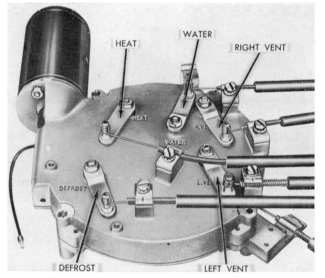

FIG. 231. In the fully automatic type of hot water heater, controls are positioned by this servo unit.

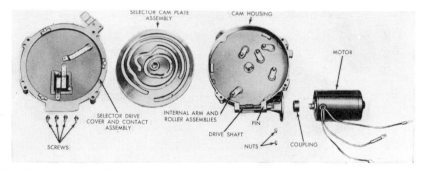

FIG. 232. Disassembled view of servo unit, showing cam mechanism which positions controls.

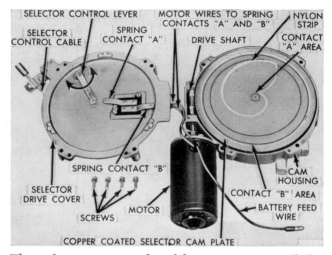

Fɪɢ. 233. The nylon strip is used to lift spring contacts "A" and "B" to stop drive motor when selector cam is in correct position as desired by driver.

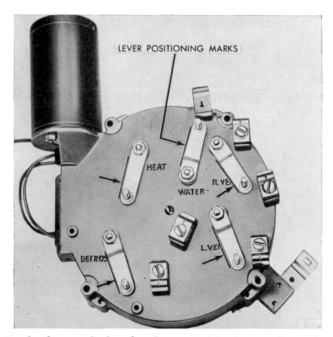

Fɪɢ. 234. Back of control plate has lever-positioning marks so that Bowden cables can be adjusted to their correct lengths.

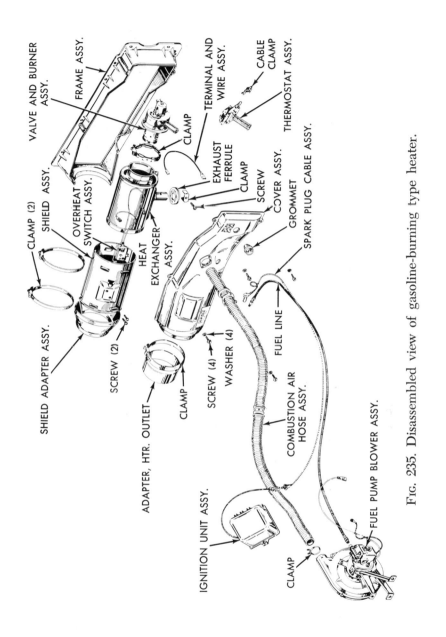

FIG. 235. Disassembled view of gasoline-burning type heater.

electrical circuit is completed, forcing air around the heat exchanger. The heated air is then blown into the car. The heater system continues in operation until the temperature at the heater duct rises slightly higher than the thermostat setting. At which time, the thermostat opens, shutting off the unit.

Service Procedures:

1. To remove the blower and fuel pump assembly, disconnect the fuel line from the pump, remove the air hose, and disconnect the blower ground wire and hot lead from the ignition unit. Loosen, but do not remove, the mounting bracket clamp. The pump and blower can now be removed by unhooking the clamps from the mounting bracket.

2. Inspect the fuel pump for evidence of leakage around the cover. Tighten the screws securely if leakage is indicated. Inspect the rubber coupling between the fuel pump and motor. Replace the coupling if it is worn or too soft. If the pump is defective, replace the entire unit. When removing or replacing the coupling connectors on the fuel pump shaft and motor shaft, remember that both shafts have left hand threads.

3. To remove the heater assembly, disconnect the combustion air hose and fuel line at the burner blower assembly. Disconnect the two wires from the terminal strip on the outside of the heater case. Remove the exhaust tube clamp and disconnect the heater exhaust tube. Remove the outlet adapter clamp at the outlet of the heater. Remove the screws which attach the cover of the heater case to the frame. The cover can now be removed with all the heater components attached.

4. To remove the burner assembly, disconnect the white and black wires from the terminals of the solenoid fuel valve and pull the ignition cable off the spark plug. Disconnect the fuel line from the fitting on the burner casting. The fuel line and ignition cable should not be removed from the grommet in the cover unless one or the other requires replacement. Loosen the clamp attaching the burner assembly to the heat exchanger and break the seal formed by the gasket. The burner assembly can now be removed with the rubber vent tube attached.

5. The nozzle and mixer assembly should receive a special inspection before disassembly since the condition of these parts will give an indication of the cause of unsatisfactory operation. The nozzle, and the inside of the mixer container around the nozzle, will nor-

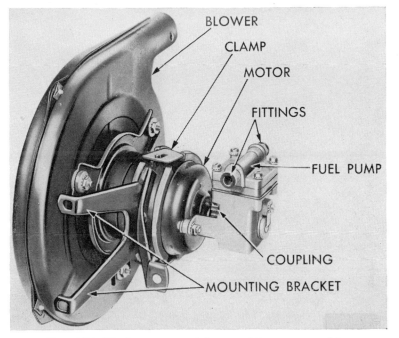

FIG. 236. Fuel pump and burner-blower assembly.

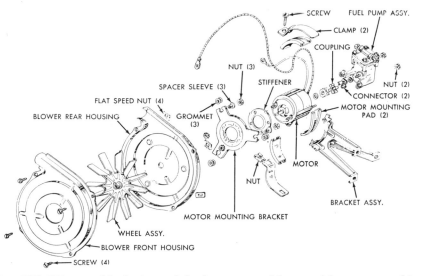

FIG. 237. Disassembled view of fuel pump and burner-blower assembly.

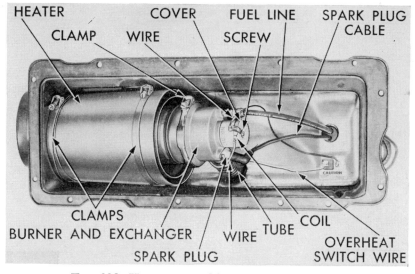

HEATER　　　　COVER　FUEL LINE　SPARK PLUG
　CLAMP　WIRE　　SCREW　　　CABLE

CLAMPS
BURNER AND EXCHANGER　WIRE　TUBE　COIL
　　　　SPARK PLUG　　　　OVERHEAT
　　　　　　　　　　　　　SWITCH WIRE

Fig. 238. Heater assembly removed from car.

mally be covered with a medium layer of black carbon and the nozzle should have a small gray area around the orifice. The outer end of the mixer will usually be burned to a gray or reddish color and some scaling or loose particles are usually present. These do no harm.

Indications of improper operation are an uneven build-up of black carbon or an excessively burned or eroded spot on the mixer. The openings around the nozzle must not be clogged with carbon since this will prevent entry of the proper amount of air. These symptoms are caused by a one-sided spray from the nozzle or by dripping or leakage around the nozzle seat.

The spark plug electrodes will operate properly with a considerable accumulation of carbon and lead but must not be shorted out. Burned electrodes are caused by an improperly directed spray; the nozzle or nozzle seat is at fault.

6. To disassemble the unit, remove the fuel fitting and screen from the fuel inlet. Remove the spark plug retaining cap and lift out the spark plug. Remove the mixer and louver plate assembly. Remove the nozzle with a ⅝ inch socket and remove the rubber spacer which is underneath.

7. Remove the solenoid cover, the coil, and the cork gasket. Then remove the three screws in the bottom of the cup and remove the cup, sealing disk, and gasket from the burner casting. Invert the

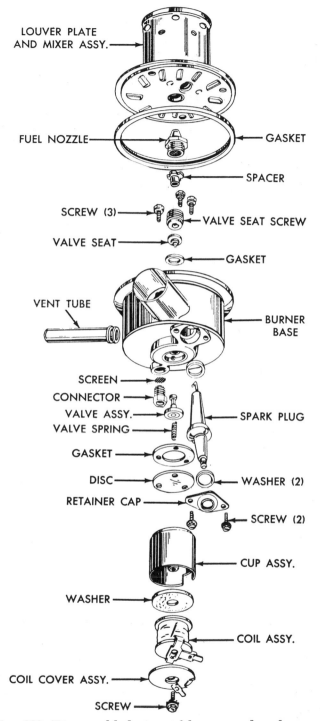

LOUVER PLATE
AND MIXER ASSY.

FUEL NOZZLE

GASKET

SPACER

SCREW (3)

VALVE SEAT SCREW

VALVE SEAT

GASKET

VENT TUBE

BURNER
BASE

SCREEN

CONNECTOR

VALVE ASSY.

SPARK PLUG

VALVE SPRING

GASKET

DISC

WASHER (2)

RETAINER CAP

SCREW (2)

CUP ASSY.

WASHER

COIL ASSY.

COIL COVER ASSY.

SCREW

FIG. 239. Disassembled view of burner and exchanger.

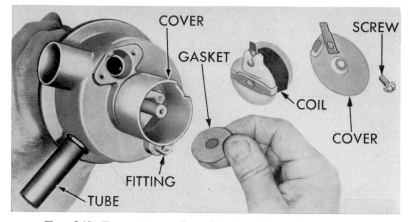

Fig. 240. Removing coil and gasket from burner unit.

casting and the valve spring and plunger will drop out. Remove the valve seat retainer from the nozzle side of the casting, using an Allen wrench (¼ inch) and remove the valve seat and gasket.

8. Inspect the valve seat for scoring around the sealing surface and inspect the end of the plunger. The plunger contains a rubber insert which must be flat and slightly recessed into the metal retainer. If the insert is uneven, replace the plunger assembly.

9. Do not attempt to clean or repair the nozzle. Replace this unit at each overhaul. Clean the burner casting, mixer assembly, and spark plug, being very careful not to permit any foreign matter to enter the passages of the burner casting. Replace defective parts.

10. To reassemble the burner, install a new screen, the fuel inlet fitting, the valve seat gasket, the valve seat, and the valve seat retainer in the order named; make sure that the pointed side of the valve seat is toward the solenoid end of the casting. Tighten the retainer firmly but do not use force. Install a new spacer and nozzle. Tighten securely.

11. Insert the valve plunger in the other end of the casting and check for free movement. Place the spring, gasket, sealing disk, and solenoid cup on the casting and reinstall the screws. Tighten evenly to insure a good seal.

12. Insert the coil retainer gasket in the bottom of the coil retainer. Insert the coil assembly so that the terminal fits down into the cut-out portion of the retainer, and the ground terminal is directly over the screw hole at the top. Install the cover on the retainer and tighten the screw securely. Position the gasket over the louver plate.

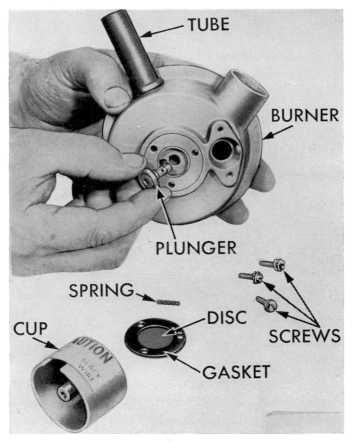

Fig. 241. Removing plunger from burner unit.

13. Position the louver plate and mixer assembly with its gasket over the nozzle. Align the screw holes and spark plug holes with their respective holes in the burner casting. Install the screws in the louver plate and tighten them finger tight. Then tighten the screws firmly and evenly.

14. Install the spark plug gaskets on the spark plug with the concave side of the gaskets against the ball portion. Carefully insert the spark plug through the louver plate. Make certain that the guide slot of the spark plug is in line with the guide on the casting. Tighten the spark plug cap attaching screws evenly and securely. Using an 0.085″ feeler gauge, adjust the spark plug gap by bending the ground electrode. Fit the rubber vent tube into the opening in the burner casting.

15. Do not remove the heat exchanger unless it is defective and

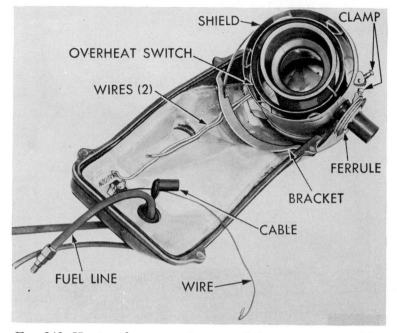

Fig. 242. Heat exchanger unit removed from cover assembly.

needs to be replaced or the overheat switch requires service. The heat exchanger has no operating parts and should require replacement only after long use.

16. If replacement should become necessary, loosen the two clamps inside the cover of the heater housing and work the exhaust ferrule free. Be careful not to bend the mounting brackets. Spread the shield assembly by hand and let the heat exchanger slide out from the straight end. The overheat switch can be removed from inside the shield. When installing the heat exchanger and shield, direct the wires below the bracket.

17. Inspect the heat exchanger for evidence of leakage, dents, and loose seams. The inside of the heat exchanger will normally contain a deposit of lead and other products of combustion but this should not be regarded as a defect unless the coating is sufficient to cause a noticeable increase in the warm-up period of the heater. When such is the case, the heater can be restored to its original efficiency by installing a new heat exchanger.

18. Inspect the overheat switch in the heat exchanger shield for broken porcelain, burned or broken wiring, loose or broken contact points, or other visible damage.

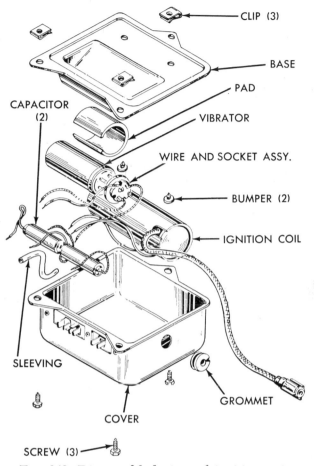

CLIP (3)

BASE

PAD

CAPACITOR (2)

VIBRATOR

WIRE AND SOCKET ASSY.

BUMPER (2)

IGNITION COIL

SLEEVING

GROMMET

COVER

SCREW (3)

FIG. 243. Disassembled view of ignition unit.

19. If the thermostat fails to control the duct outlet temperature, it is usually an indication that the cam is loose on the helix shaft or the end of the helix has dropped out of the slot in the control shaft. To correct this condition, adjust the thermostat as follows:

Remove the thermostat and inspect the helix to make sure it is crimped tightly in the end of the control shaft. With the helix at room temperature, loosen the Allen setscrew in the plastic cam on the base end of the control shaft, making sure the shaft is completely free to revolve and take its normal position at room temperature (about 75° to 85°F.). With the plastic cam free on the shaft and the micro-switch *down,* move the control cable linkage as far as it will go to the *left* and hold it in this position. While holding the linkage, turn the plastic cam in a counterclockwise direction until

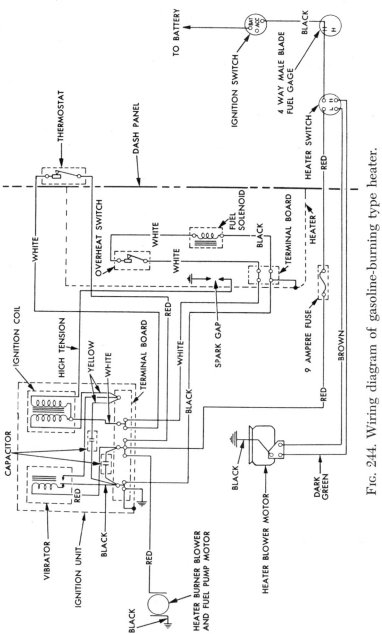

Fig. 244. Wiring diagram of gasoline-burning type heater.

the micro-switch just clicks, then tighten the setscrew in the cam. Be careful not to disturb the two screws which attach the micro-switch to the thermostat base.

20. When reinstalling the thermostat, insert the control cable and housing through the retainer clip located on the upper portion of the thermostat mounting plate. Insert the end of the cable through the swivel holes of the thermostat linkage, but do not tighten the screw. Move the temperature control to the extreme *low heat* position; then move the thermostat control linkage in a *downward* direction as far as it will go. Tighten the swivel screw. When the thermostat cable is properly installed, the temperature control should move the thermostat linkage from one extreme to the other without interference from the cable housing.

21. In the event of ignition failure, that has been traced to the ignition unit, it will be necessary to determine which component is responsible. This is easily done by first substituting a vibrator that is known to be good. If the trouble is eliminated, the old vibrator was at fault. If substitution of the vibrator fails to correct the difficulty, the ignition coil is probably at fault. Capacitor failure will usually lead to failure of the vibrator through pitting of the points and new capacitors should always be installed when the vibrator is changed. Failure of the capacitor may also be indicated by noise in the car radio.

22. To gain access to the ignition unit components, remove the mounting screws and then remove the clips through which the screws were installed. The cover of the unit can then be removed for servicing.

TROUBLESHOOTING

TROUBLES	CAUSES
1. No heat or not enough heat	1a. With the ignition switch and the heater switch *on*, the fresh air blower and the burner blower motor and fuel pump assembly should start immediately; otherwise, there is a defective heater switch, fuse, or wiring.
	1b. A defective coupling between the motor and fuel pump will cause loss of fuel pressure even if the motor is running.

TROUBLESHOOTING—(Continued)

TROUBLES	CAUSES

1c. Check the ground and the voltage at the red terminal of the ignition unit with a test light. If the test light goes *on,* replace the burner blower motor.

1d. If both blowers run, touch the white lead to the white terminal. A click should be heard as the fuel control valve opens and closes with the temperature control in the *HIGH HEAT* position.

1e. If the valve fails to click, shut off the ignition and install a jumper wire between the white terminal inside the heater case and the white terminal of the solenoid valve. Disconnect the overheat switch wires from the terminals but leave all other wires connected. Temporarily replace the cover of the heater case and turn on the ignition switch. Recheck the fuel control valve.

1f. If the valve fails to click with the overheat switch shorted out, check the voltage at the white lead with a test light or meter. If the lead is hot, and the valve fails to click with the overheat switch shorted out, the fuel valve solenoid coil is defective. **CAUTION:** *Do not permit the white lead to be grounded while making these tests.*

1g. If the solenoid valve is operating properly, check the ignition unit. Turn off the ignition switch. Separate the two sections of the ignition cable at the connector. Insert an automotive type plug in the end of the ignition unit section of the ignition cable and ground the plug to the body of the car. Adjust the gap to 0.085″. Turn the

TROUBLESHOOTING—(Continued)

TROUBLES   CAUSES

ignition and heater switches *on* and check the plug for a hot spark. If there is no spark, the ignition unit is defective and must be replaced or repaired.

1h. If there is a spark at the plug, reconnect the ignition cable and check the fuel pressure with a *T* fitting and a gauge at the outlet of the fuel pump while the car engine is running. The pressure should be 21 to 23 psi. If the pressure is satisfactory, and the heater does not ignite, the nozzle is clogged or the spark plug shorted out and the burner assembly must be removed from the heater for further tests. Fuel pressure as high as 27 psi is an indication of a clogged nozzle.

1i. To examine the spray pattern, connect the white lead (removed from the front of the case) directly to the insulated terminal of the valve solenoid. Disconnect the ignition cable from the spark plug. Connect the black lead to the ground terminal. At the ignition unit, disconnect both white wires and clip them together using tape to insulate the connection. These wiring connections will energize the solenoid directly without going through the overheat switch. Start the engine and turn the heater switch *on*. The fuel valve will open and the spray from the nozzle can then be examined.

CAUTION: *Have a fire extinguisher at hand and avoid any possibility of igniting the spray.* The spray pattern must consist of a fine mist of fuel which is symmetrical in shape

TROUBLESHOOTING—(Continued)

and is centered in the mixer assembly. There must be no dripping or leakage around the nozzle seat. If the spray is coarse or uneven, or is directed at an angle in the mixer, the nozzle is defective.

1j. Additional causes of burner failure are excessive clogging of the screen in the fuel inlet, clogging of the fuel passages within the burner casting, or a defective valve plunger or seat.

2. Heater gets too hot

2a. This condition can be caused by a poorly adjusted thermostat or insufficient fresh air.

2b. To test the thermostat, connect a test light between the white terminal of the ignition unit and ground. Start the heater with the engine running. After the heater warms up, the test light should go *on* and *off* as the thermostat cycles.

2c. If the heater cycles, but the test light remains on, it is an indication that the thermostat contacts are remaining closed and the heater is cycling on the overheat switch. Install a new thermostat.

2d. The fresh air supply should be checked before replacing the thermostat since proper thermostat action is dependent on an adequate supply of fresh air.

2e. An insufficient air flow can be caused by a defective fresh air blower motor or by an obstruction in the fresh air system. The fresh air door must be *closed* and the temperature control arm moved to a position between *ON* and *WARMER*.

3. Heater works intermittently

3a. If the heater gets very hot and shuts itself *on* and *off* in an intermittent way, the trouble is

TROUBLESHOOTING—(Continued)

TROUBLES	CAUSES
	probably caused by an insufficient fresh air flow.
	3b. Intermittent operation may also be caused by an air lock in the heater fuel pump. Bleed the fuel line to remove air bubbles.
4. Heater causes odor	4a. If the odor is raw gasoline, the fuel connection at the burner casting is leaking or the solenoid valve is not tight.
	4b. If the odor is burned gasoline, the exhaust tube under the heater is leaking and must be repaired.
5. Too much smoke from the heater	5a. Excessive smoking and carbon are caused by a slow air motor or a defective nozzle.
	5b. This condition could also be caused by a delayed ignition, resulting from a defective spark plug.
6. Heater makes noise when starting	6a. If the heater "pops" or "spits" when starting or cycling, a leaking solenoid valve seat or plunger is permitting fuel to flow in the *off* position.
	6b. Another cause is low fuel pressure from a defective pump or insufficient air caused by a slow blower motor.

AIR CONDITIONING

Introduction. Control of temperature, relative humidity, and air movement are required to satisfy personal comfort. The importance of removing excessive heat is quite well known, but it is equally important to control the relative humidity because discomfort results from too much moisture in the air. The body moisture is not absorbed at a satisfactory rate to produce a sense of well being. It is the task of an air conditioning unit to cool the air, remove excess moisture, and clean the air of dirt and dust.

All air conditioning systems operate on either outside or recirculated inside air; or on a combination of both. The air is dehumidified and cooled as it passes through the evaporator coil and then reheated to the desired temperature as it passes through the heater core. The

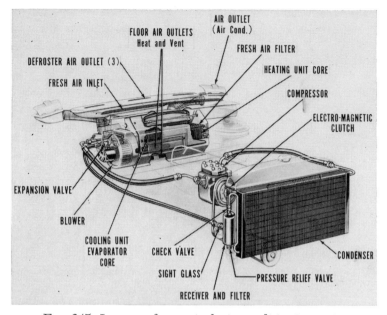

FIG. 245. Layout of a typical air-conditioning unit.

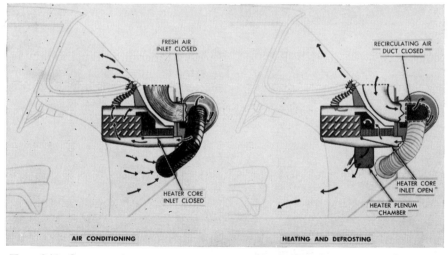

FIG. 246. Some units contain provisions for repositioning vent doors so that unit works on recirculated or fresh air.

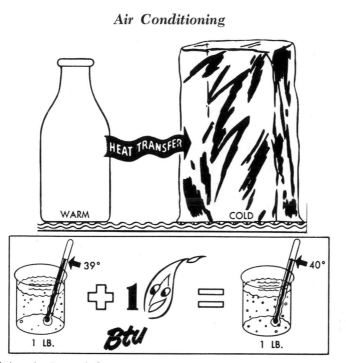

FIG. 247 (*top*). One of the principles of heat transfer is that heat always travels from a warm object to a cooler one.

FIG. 248 (*bottom*). A BTU (British Thermal Unit) is the amount of heat required to raise the temperature of 1 lb. of water 1°F.

amount of reheat added to the air is controlled by metering hot water through the heater core. The reheat feature dehumidifies the air because dust and dirt adhere to the damp surfaces of the cooling coils and are discharged through the drain along with the condensate.

Principles of Refrigeration. Refrigeration is the process of removing heat.

All matter exists in either a solid, liquid, or a gaseous state. The physical form or state of any substance depends entirely on the amount of heat that it contains. Many substances can be readily converted from one physical state to another by the addition or removal of heat. A familiar example is the change of water into either steam or ice.

Heat can be measured in two ways—*intensity* and *quantity*. The intensity is measured with a thermometer in units, called degrees. The standard of measurement for quantity is known as the British Thermal Unit, commonly called BTU which is defined as the amount of heat required to raise the temperature of 1 pound of water 1 degree Fahrenheit. The difference between intensity and quantity may be illustrated with 2 containers filled with 1 and 2 pounds of water respectively, each at the same temperature, or intensity. There are twice as many heat units (quantity) in the 2 pound container as in the one pound container because it will take twice as long to raise the temperature (intensity) of 2 pounds of water the same number of degrees as 1 pound of water.

There are two kinds of heat called *sensible* and *latent*. Sensible heat is the heat that changes the temperature of a substance with no change in the form. Latent heat is the heat that changes the form of a substance without changing its temperature. For example, if water is heated anywhere below the boiling point, the absorbed sensible heat will cause the temperature to rise until the boiling point is reached. At this point, additional latent heat will be absorbed to convert the water to a vapor but the temperature will remain at 212°F.

All liquids have a definite boiling point, which is dependent on the pressure applied. Water, for example, will boil at 212°F. only at sea level atmospheric pressure. If the pressure is increased, the liquid will not boil until a higher temperature is reached. Thus Freon-12, which normally boils at 21.7°F. below zero, if exposed to the atmosphere, can be prevented from boiling if it is kept under high pressure. Conversely, if the pressure is decreased, the liquid will boil at a lower temperature.

A definite pressure and temperature relationship exists in the case of liquid refrigerants and their saturated vapors. Increasing the temperature of a substance causes it to expand. When this substance is confined in a closed container, an increase in temperature will be accompanied by an increase in pressure, even though no mechanical device is used. For every variation in temperature, there will be a corresponding pressure variation within the container of refrigerant.

When a liquid boils, turning into a vapor, it absorbs a great amount of latent heat without changing temperature. This heat is known as *latent heat of vaporization*. Conversely, when the vapor is condensed, the process is reversed and the same amount of heat is released in converting the vapor to liquid. The principle of large heat absorption or release that occurs when a liquid changes its state is the basis of a modern refrigeration system.

The term *hot* is not necessarily associated with a boiling liquid. Freon-12, the refrigerant used in air conditioning systems, boils at 21.7°F. *below* zero. Thus, if it were exposed to the air at normal

TEMPERATURE AND PRESSURE RELATION CHART FOR REFRIGERANT 12

Temp. F.	Press. of Refrig.	Temp. F.	Press. of Refrig.	Temp. F.	Press. of Refrig.	Temp. F.	Press. of Refrig.
0	9.1	43	39.7	76	78.3	109	135.1
2	10.1	44	40.7	77	79.2	110	136.0
4	11.2	45	41.7	78	81.1	111	138.0
6	12.3	46	42.6	79	82.5	112	140.1
8	13.4	47	43.6	80	84.0	113	142.1
10	14.6	48	44.6	81	85.5	114	144.2
12	15.8	49	45.6	82	87.0	115	146.3
14	17.1	50	46.6	83	88.5	116	148.4
16	18.3	51	47.8	84	90.1	117	151.2
18	19.7	52	48.7	85	91.7	118	152.7
20	21.0	53	49.8	86	93.2	119	154.9
21	21.7	54	50.9	87	94.8	120	157.1
22	22.4	55	52.0	88	96.4	121	159.3
23	23.1	56	53.1	89	98.0	122	161.5
24	23.8	57	55.4	90	99.6	123	163.8
25	24.6	58	56.6	91	101.3	124	166.1
26	25.3	59	57.1	92	103.0	125	168.4
27	26.1	60	57.7	93	104.6	126	170.7
28	26.8	61	58.9	94	106.3	127	173.1
29	27.6	62	60.0	95	108.1	128	175.4
30	28.4	63	61.3	96	109.8	129	177.8
31	29.2	64	62.5	97	111.5	130	182.2
32	30.0	65	63.7	98	113.3	131	182.6
33	30.9	66	64.9	99	115.1	132	185.1
34	31.7	67	66.2	100	116.9	133	187.6
35	32.5	68	67.5	101	118.8	134	190.1
36	33.4	69	68.8	102	120.6	135	192.6
37	34.3	70	70.1	103	122.4	136	195.2
38	35.1	71	71.4	104	124.3	137	197.8
39	36.0	72	72.8	105	126.2	138	200.0
40	36.9	73	74.2	106	128.1	139	209.2
41	37.9	74	75.5	107	130.0	140	205.5
42	38.8	75	76.9	108	132.1		

room temperature, it would absorb heat and boil, immediately changing into a vapor.

Saturated vapor is vapor which is in contact with its liquid and which is at the same temperature as the boiling point of its liquid. It will remain saturated as long as it is in contact with its liquid. All vapors used in refrigeration systems are saturated vapors.

Superheated vapor is a vapor which has its temperature increased above the boiling point of the liquid from which it came.

Compressing a vapor increases its temperature, and, conversely, expanding a vapor decreases its temperature. A tire pump, for example, will become warm when pumping air into a tire due to the heating of the air when being compressed. Any vapor can be liquefied by squeezing or compressing it if sufficient pressure is exerted.

Pressure-Temperature Relationship of Freon. The chart shows that every time the temperature of Freon is changed, the pressure is also changed. Unfortunately, the change is not in the same ratio. If the temperature of the refrigerant is known, the pressure-temperature chart will show what the pressure should be. (See page 201.)

Theory of Operation:

High-Pressure Side. With the control switch *on,* the thermostat calling for refrigeration, and the engine and compressor in operation, low-pressure vapor is changed into high-pressure vapor by the compressor and discharged into the condenser. The vapor changes into liquid in the condenser and then flows into the top of the receiver-dehydrator, where it is stored and the moisture removed. The liquid is forced through the high-pressure line which connects to the sight glass, and then on to the high-pressure side of the expansion valve.

Low-Pressure Side. At the orifice of the expansion valve, the high-pressure liquid changes into a low-pressure liquid due to the vacuum developed at the inlet side of the compressor. From here it enters the cooling coil. As the refrigerant enters this low-pressure area, it begins to boil thus absorbing heat from the walls of the cooling coils. Because the cooling coil is colder than the air surrounding it, some of the passenger car compartment heat passes through the walls of the refrigerated tubes into the liquid refrigerant. The resulting low-pressure vapor is drawn back to the compressor where the cycle starts over again.

Parts of the System:

Clutch and Pulley Assembly. The clutch and pulley assembly, which is mounted in front of the compressor, is driven by a "V" belt. The clutch is magnetically operated by a clutch actuating coil and armature and operates the compressor when refrigeration is required.

Compressor. The compressor is used to pressurize the system and keep the refrigerant in motion. Chrysler and Ford use a two-cylinder compressor while General Motors uses a five-cylinder pump. In both cases, reed-type valves are used to control the flow of refrigerant.

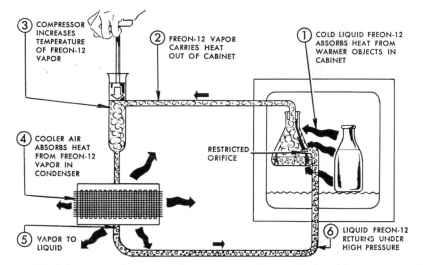

FIG. 249. Schematic diagram of operation of a typical refrigeration unit.

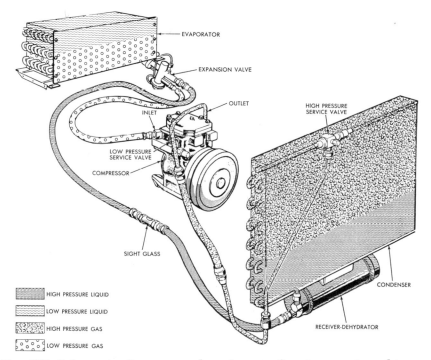

FIG. 250. Schematic diagram to show layout of various parts making up
a typical air-conditioning unit.

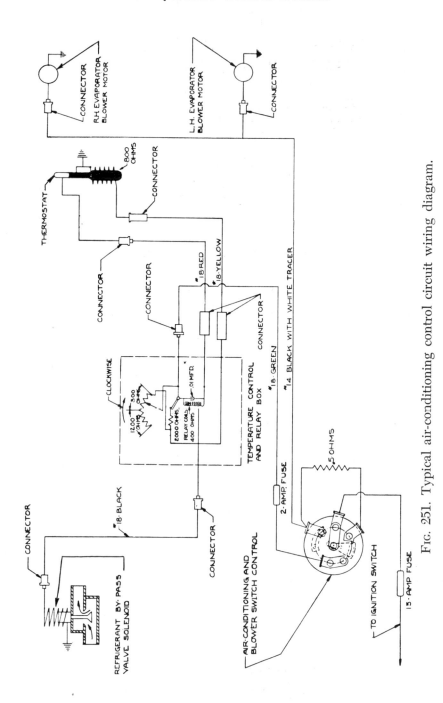

FIG. 251. Typical air-conditioning control circuit wiring diagram.

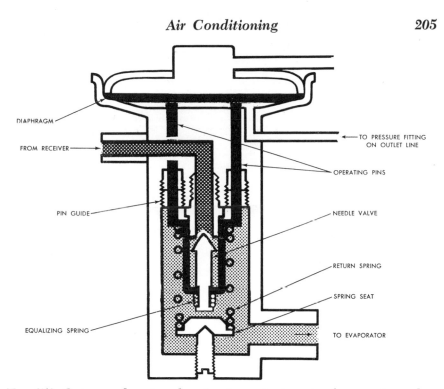

FIG. 252. Cutaway drawing showing important parts of expansion valve.

Condenser. The condenser contains two oval refrigerant tubes which form a continuous path for the refrigerant vapor. The adjacent passages are joined by a corrugated finned strip which serves to increase the effective radiation surface.

The condenser is located in front of the radiator and mounted to the radiator support.

Receiver-Dehydrator. The receiver, which serves as a reservoir for storage of high-pressure liquid produced in the condenser, incorporates a dehydrating agent which is held in the lower portion of the receiver between two screens.

The function of the dehydrator is to absorb any moisture that may have escaped removal during service operations. *The importance of keeping the interior of the system free of moisture cannot be overemphasized.*

Expansion Valve. The expansion valve is a thermostatically controlled needle and seat. Its purpose is to regulate the flow of liquid refrigerant according to the requirements of the evaporator (cooling coil).

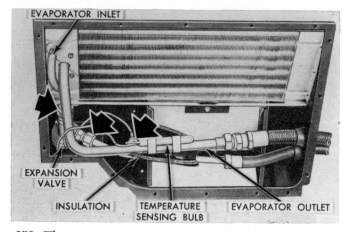

EVAPORATOR INLET

EXPANSION VALVE

INSULATION   TEMPERATURE SENSING BULB   EVAPORATOR OUTLET

FIG. 253. The evaporator unit. Arrows point to expansion valve connections.

Refrigeration begins at the needle seat (orifice) which is the pressure dividing point of the valve. High-pressure liquid enters the valve from the receiver-dehydrator and passes on to the seat orifice. Low-pressure liquid leaves the orifice and flows into the evaporator coil. The low-pressure liquid absorbs heat from the coil and changes into a low-pressure gas.

A power element controls the quantity of liquid that is being metered through the expansion valve. As the temperature of the low-pressure line changes at the bulb, the pressure of the vapor in the power element changes, resulting in a change of the position of the needle. For example, if the cooling coil gets more liquid than is needed, the temperature of the low-pressure line is reduced, and the resulting lowering of the bulb temperature reduces the pressure of the vapor in the power element allowing the needle to move closer to its seat. This immediately reduces the amount of liquid leaving the valve.

Evaporator. The evaporator is a housing containing the cooling coil assembly (evaporator), the thermostatic expansion valve, and the blower motor. This unit is joined to the heater core where the proper reheat is added to the refrigerated air.

Sight Glass. The sight glass provides a quick and sure way of determining if the refrigerant charge is sufficient. A shortage of refrigerant causes bubbles and foam to appear beneath the glass. It is a valuable addition to the system when troubleshooting.

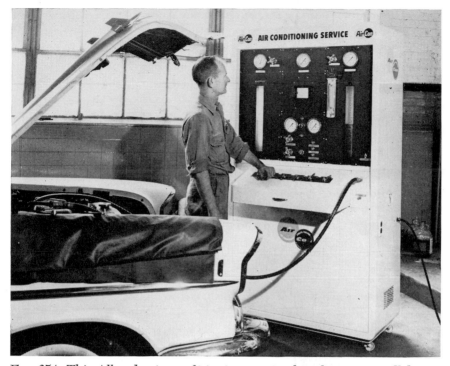

Fɪɢ. 254. This Allstadt air-conditioning service bench contains all hoses, gauges, a tank of Freon, and scales to service air-conditioning systems.

The sight glass is located in the high-pressure liquid line at the receiver-dehydrator outlet.

Service Procedures:

General. In removing and replacing any part, the system must be *depressurized.* After the part is replaced, the system must be *evacuated* to remove all traces of old refrigerant and moisture. Then the system is *recharged* with new refrigerant.

If only the compressor needs service or replacement, the rest of the system need not be depressurized or evacuated because the service valves on top of the compressor can be closed to isolate it from the rest of the system.

Precautions in Handling Freon. Freon is a transparent and colorless refrigerant in both the gaseous and liquid states. It has a boiling point of 21.7°F. below zero and, therefore, at all normal temperatures and pressures it is a vapor. The vapor is heavier than air and is noninflammable, nonexplosive, nonpoisonous (except when in contact with an open flame), and noncorrosive (except when in contact with water). The following precautions in handling Freon should be observed at all times:

1. All refrigerant drums are shipped with a heavy metal screw cap. The purpose of the cap is to protect the valve and safety plug from damage. Replace the cap after each use of the drum.

2. If it is necessary to transport a drum or can of refrigerant in a car, keep it in the luggage compartment. It should never be exposed to the radiant heat of the sun because the resulting increase in pressure may cause the safety plug or the drum to burst.

3. Drums or disposable cans should never be subjected to excessively high temperatures when adding refrigerant to the system. In most instances, heating the drum or can is required to raise the pressure in the container higher than the pressure in the system. It would be unwise to place the drum on a gas stove while preparing for the charging operation, because a serious accident can result. Don't depend on the safety plug—the drum may burst if the safety plug should fail. A bucket of warm water, not over 125°F., or warm wet rags around the container is all the heat that is needed. Welding or steam cleaning near a refrigeration system can result in a dangerous buildup of pressure.

4. When filling a small drum from a large one, never fill the drum completely. Space should always be allowed above the liquid for expansion. If the drum were completely filled and the temperature increased, hydraulic pressure would exert a tremendous force.

5. Discharging large quantities of Freon into the shop usually can be done with safety as the vapors produce no ill effects. However, this should not be done if the area contains a flame. While Freon normally is nonpoisonous, heavy concentrations of it in contact with a live flame will produce a toxic gas. This gas will attack bright metal surfaces.

6. Protection of your eyes is of vital importance! An accident, when working around high-pressure lines, may cause the refrigerant to spray into your face. Protect your eyes with safety glasses. Remember, that any Freon liquid that touches you is at least 21.7°F. *below* zero. The eyeballs cannot take very much of this temperature. If an accident should occur, and Freon gets into your eyes, here is what to do:

a. Keep calm.
b. Do not rub the eyes.

c. Splash the affected area with quantities of cold water to get the temperature above the freezing point.

d. Use a film of mineral, cod liver, or an antiseptic oil to provide protection and reduce the possibility of infection.

e. As soon as possible, call a doctor or an eye specialist.

Precautions in Handling Refrigerant Lines:

1. All metal tubing lines should be free of kinks, because of the restriction that kinks offer to the flow of refrigerant. The capacity of the entire system can be greatly reduced by a single kink.

2. The flexible hose lines should never be bent to a radius of less than ten times the diameter of the hose.

3. The flexible hose lines should never be allowed to come within a distance of 2″ of the exhaust manifold.

4. Flexible hose lines should be inspected at least once a year for leaks or brittleness. Damaged hoses should be replaced immediately.

5. Use only sealed and dehydrated lines from parts stock.

6. The use of the proper wrenches, when making connections, is very important. The opposing fitting should always be backed up with a wrench to prevent distortion of the connecting lines or components. When connecting the flexible hose connections, it is important, that the swaged fitting and the flare nut, as well as the coupling to which it is attached, be held at the same time using three different wrenches to prevent turning the fitting and damaging the ground seat.

7. Flares and flare seats should be coated with refrigeration oil before they are assembled to permit the flares to seat squarely and provide for proper tightening. Special thread sealer for refrigerant systems is available.

8. When disconnecting any fitting, the system must first be discharged of all pressure. However, proceed cautiously regardless of gauge readings. Open a fitting very slowly, keeping your face and hands as far away as possible, so that no injury can occur if there happens to be liquid in the line. If pressure is noticed, allow it to bleed off very slowly.

CAUTION: *Always wear safety goggles when opening refrigerant lines.*

9. Any newly opened line should be capped immediately to prevent the entrance of moisture or dirt.

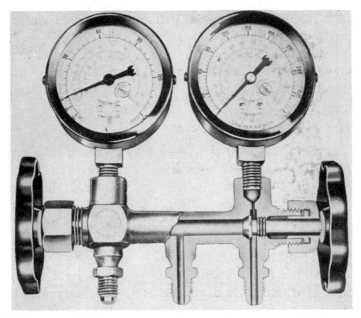

FIG. 255. The manifold gauge set with one side cut away to show passages from valve to gauge.

10. Flares and flare seats must be in perfect condition. The slightest burr or piece of dirt may cause a leak.

Manifold Gauge Set. The manifold gauge set is used when evacuating, charging, and troubleshooting the air-conditioning system.

The gauge on the left is the low-pressure gauge and is used to check pressure on the low-pressure side of the system. It is graduated in inches of vacuum from 0 to 30 and in pounds per square inch, from 0 to 150 psi.

The gauge on the right is the high-pressure gauge and is used for checking the pressure on the high-pressure side of the system. The gauge is graduated from 0 to 300 pounds pressure per square inch.

The connection on the left is for attaching the low-pressure gauge line; the one on the right is for attaching the high-pressure gauge line. The connection in the center is for the purpose of attaching a line for evacuating or charging the system. When this connection is not required, it must be capped.

The valves are opened and closed by means of handles at each end of the manifold. At no time is it possible to close off the gauges. The valves merely close off the center connection from each end

Fɪɢ. 256. Location of low- (suction) and high-pressure (discharge) valves on top of compressor.

connection and from one another. When the valves are turned all the way in (fully clockwise), the center connection is closed to both sides of the system. When the valves are turned all the way out (fully counterclockwise), both valves are open to the center connection and to the system pressure valves. When the gauge lines are first connected, they contain some air. It is necessary, therefore, to bleed the lines before pressure readings are taken. To bleed the lines, turn both manifold gauge valves fully clockwise. Attach the gauge lines to the service valves and tighten them securely. Leave both gauge lines loose at the manifold fitting. "Crack" the low-pressure service valve until escaping gas can be heard at the loose manifold fitting, and then tighten it securely. Then bleed the high-pressure valve in the same way.

When checking operating pressures, it is a good idea to open the service valves not over ¼ turn. A slight opening dampens compressor pulsations. If the gauge needle still flutters, close the valve slowly until the fluttering stops.

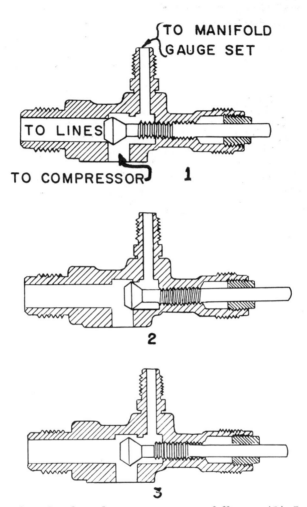

FIG. 257. Each valve has three positions as follows: (1) Isolating the compressor, valve fully frontseated—fully clockwise; (2) normal operation, valve fully backseated—fully counterclockwise; (3) position for connecting manifold gauge set so that Freon can be added, valve "cracked open."

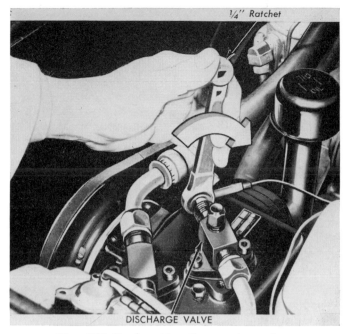

Fig. 258. Backseating the service valve.

Summary of Gauge and Valve Settings:

Settings of the Manifold Gauge Valves	Settings of the Compressor Service Valves
System in Operation	
Not used.	Both valves backseated—fully counterclockwise.
Isolating the Compressor for Removal	
Not used.	Both valves frontseated—fully clockwise.
Measuring Pressure in the System	
Both valves closed—fully clockwise.	Both valves "cracked open"—about ¼ turn clockwise.
Depressurizing the System	
Center connection—cap removed. Both valves "cracked open"—slightly counterclockwise.	Both valves open to midpoint—about 3 turns from either end position.
Evacuating the System—Vacuum Pump Method	
Center connection—connected to vacuum pump.	

Settings of the Manifold Gauge Valves	Settings of the Compressor Service Valves

EVACUATING THE SYSTEM—VACUUM PUMP METHOD—(*Continued*)

Low-pressure valve open—fully counterclockwise.	Low-pressure valve open to midpoint—about 3 turns from either end position.
High-pressure valve closed—fully clockwise.	High-pressure valve backseated—fully counterclockwise.

EVACUATING THE SYSTEM—CAR COMPRESSOR METHOD

Center connection—not used.	
Low-pressure valve closed—fully clockwise.	Low-pressure valve open to midpoint—about 3 turns from either end position.
High-pressure valve—not used.	High-pressure valve frontseated—fully clockwise.

ADDING REFRIGERANT

Center connection—connected to Freon drum.	
Low-pressure valve open—fully counterclockwise.	Low-pressure valve open to midpoint—about 3 turns from either end position.
High-pressure valve closed—fully clockwise.	High-pressure valve "cracked open" —about ¼ turn clockwise.

Depressurizing the System. When replacing any of the air-conditioning components, the system must be purged or drained of refrigerant. The purpose is to lower the pressure so that a part can be removed safely.

1. With the engine stopped and the compressor service valves backseated and positioned for normal operation (fully counterclockwise), remove the air cleaner and install the high- and low-pressure lines of the gauge manifold set to the high- and low-pressure outlets on the compressor.

2. Open both service valves ¼ turn clockwise.

3. With the cap removed from the center of the gauge manifold set, open the high-pressure gauge valve and discharge the vapor slowly through the center connection. CAUTION: Do not open the valve too much or the compressor oil may be discharged with the Freon. Wrap a rag around the end of the center gauge line to prevent the splashing of oil in the event of an accidental discharge.

4. When the pressure has been reduced below 100 psi on the high-pressure gauge, open the low-pressure gauge valve and continue discharging until the pressure does not exceed 5 psi. Close both gauge valves.

5. Frontseat both service valves (fully clockwise). The compressor is now isolated, and the system is ready for parts replacement.

Evacuating the System. Whenever the air-conditioning system is opened for any reason, it must not be put back in operation until it has been evacuated to remove air and moisture which may have entered.

There are two methods which may be used to evacuate the system. The preferred method is to connect a vacuum pump to evacuate the system. If no vacuum pump is available, the car compressor can be used to evacuate the system.

Vacuum Pump Method:

1. Attach the manifold gauge set to the low- and high-pressure service valves on top of the compressor. Turn the low-pressure service valve to its midposition. Be sure that the high-pressure valve is backseated (fully counterclockwise) to prevent pulling a vacuum on the high-pressure gauge.

2. Connect the flexible hose of the manifold center connection to the vacuum pump. Open the valve to the low-pressure gauge and close the valve to the high-pressure gauge.

3. Start the vacuum pump and evacuate the system to the lowest possible vacuum. A reading of 26–28 inches should be obtained in about 10 minutes. However, the pump must be operated for an additional five minutes to make sure that all moisture has been evacuated.

If difficulty is experienced in reaching a high vacuum, check for a leak by closing the low-pressure gauge valve and stopping the pump. If the gauge does not hold its vacuum, a leak is present which must be repaired before further work is done.

4. When the system has been evacuated satisfactorily, close the low-pressure gauge valve and disconnect the vacuum pump. The system is now ready to be charged.

Compressor Method:

1. Attach the flexible hose of the low-pressure manifold gauge to the low-pressure service valve on the compressor. Turn the low-pressure service valve to its midposition.

2. Remove the cap from the high-pressure service valve port, and then frontseat the valve (fully clockwise). This will permit the system to be evacuated to the atmosphere.

3. Close the low-pressure gauge valve. Operate the engine at 450–475 rpm. Then energize the compressor magnetic clutch using a jumper wire from the battery to the clutch brush holder feed wire. Observe the vacuum gauge reading; 26–28 inches of vacuum should be reached in about 10 minutes. Operate the compressor for an additional five minutes to be sure that all moisture has been removed. **Note:** Watch the high-pressure service valve port for the presence of oil. If oil is being discharged, slow down the engine.

4. When the system has been evacuated satisfactorily, frontseat the low-pressure valve (fully clockwise), cap the high-pressure service valve port, open the circuit to the magnetic clutch, and stop the engine. The system is now ready to be charged.

Adding Refrigerant. An important rule to follow in charging the system is that refrigerant should always be added to the compressor in a vaporous state. Another important rule is never to add refrigerant until the system has been leak tested and properly processed. Refrigerant is always added to the low-pressure side of the compressor.

In order to charge refrigerant in the vapor state, the Freon drum must be kept upright to prevent the exit of liquids. The pressure may be raised in a partially empty container by heating a bucket of water to not over 125°F. and setting the Freon container in the heated water. Since the temperature of the water and drum will decrease as the vapor leaves the container, the water will be cooled. This results in a lowering of pressure to the extent that it may be necessary to reheat the water.

With the compressor in operation, the pressure should not exceed 275 psi on the high-pressure side, and the pressure within the Freon container should not be allowed to drop below 12 psi. When the low-pressure valve on the manifold gauge set is closed, the gauge indicates the low-side pressure in the compressor. When the low-pressure valve on the manifold gauge set is open, the gauge indicates drum pressure.

Consult the manufacturer's specifications for the amount of refrigerant required as it varies with car models.

Charging the System—Complete. If the entire charge of refrigerant has been lost through accident or in the replacement of any component, a complete charge will be necessary and should be added *after evacuation* as described below:

1. With the manifold gauge set and Freon container installed as shown, make sure the high- and low-pressure gauge valves and the

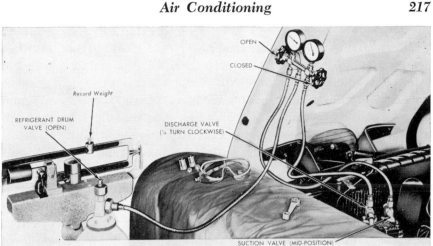

Fig. 259. Connections and positions of valves ready to charge the system.

valve on the Freon container are closed. Now, turn each compressor service valve to its maximum counterclockwise position, and then open the valve on the Freon drum.

2. Bleed the air from the manifold and hoses.

3. Place the Freon drum on the scales to weigh it accurately. This is important to determine the amount of Freon used. If a pail of heated water is used for more pressure, it must be weighed with the Freon.

4. Open the low-pressure gauge valve and set the compressor low-pressure service valve at its midpoint position. Refrigerant will enter the system under drum pressure. When the gauge reads 40 psi, leak test the system thoroughly.

5. Start the engine, turn the temperature control to the *max* position, and position the blower switch on *high* speed. Operate the engine at 1200 to 1500 rpm. To check the pressure in the high-pressure side of the system, "crack open" the high-pressure service valve. The pressure must not be allowed to go over 300 psi. If it does, shut off the engine and troubleshoot.

6. Check the weight of the refrigerant drum frequently during the charging process. When the specified weight of refrigerant has entered the system, close the valves on the low-pressure side of the manifold and refrigerant drum. Backseat both service valves to their maximum counterclockwise position.

7. Operate the system 2 minutes, and then check the sight glass. If it is clear and shows no bubbles or foaming, the system is properly charged.

8. If bubbles or foaming can be seen, operate the system for an additional 10 minutes and recheck the sight glass. If the glass has not cleared, add one pound of Freon. If the system still does not clear, it contains air or moisture. Depressurize the system, make the necessary corrections, evacuate, and recharge the system again.

9. After the system is fully charged, check to be sure that the high- and low-pressure service valves are backseated (fully counterclockwise), that the valve on top of the Freon tank is closed, and that the valve stem caps and the caps on the high- and low-pressure service valve gauge ports are replaced.

Charging the System—Partial. This operation is performed when a shortage of refrigerant is caused by leakage. Check the system for leaks and make necessary repairs. Check the compressor oil level and add oil if necessary.

1. Connect the manifold gauge set and the Freon container to the compressor as shown in Fig. 259. Both gauge valves should be closed.

2. Bleed the hoses and manifold.

3. Start the engine, turn the temperature control to the *max* position, and position the blower switch to *high* speed. Operate the system for 5 minutes at 1200–1500 rpm to stabilize it.

4. Open the low-pressure service valve to its midpoint—about 3 turns from its backseated position. "Crack open" the high-pressure service valve to obtain a reading on the high-pressure gauge.

5. Open the valve on the low-pressure side of the manifold gauge set to allow refrigerant to enter the system through the low-pressure valve of the compressor. When the bubbles disappear in the sight glass, close the valve on the low-pressure side of the manifold. Note the weight of the Freon drum. Then open the manifold valve and add an additional pound of Freon. Close the valve on the low-pressure side of the manifold.

6. Stop the engine and backseat both service valves to their maximum counterclockwise position. Close the valve on the Freon drum and remove the manifold hoses from the drum and service valve gauge ports. Install the service valve stem and gauge port caps.

Testing the Moisture Content of the System:

The importance of operating a *dry* air-conditioning system cannot be overemphasized. Excessive moisture causes the system to freeze up in cold weather and it stops operating. Even a small amount of moisture will produce Hydrofloric and Hydrochloric Acids which attack metal and produce corrosive sludge. This sludge plugs up screens, corrodes compressor reeds, and gums up the expansion valve. And when you realize that even a new drum of Freon, as delivered by the manufacturer, contains enough moisture to play havoc with an air-conditioning system, the importance of checking for, and removing excess moisture becomes apparent.

1. Connect the tubing coil, sight glass, moisture detecting eye and cap into an assembly. Remove the valve stem caps from the low-

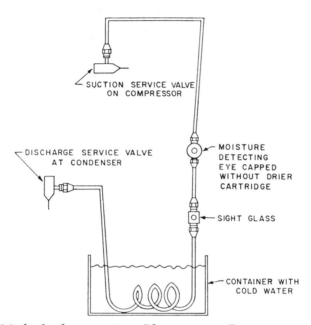

F ig. 260. Method of connecting "detecting eye" into system to detect presence of moisture.

and high-pressure service valves. Fully backseat (counterclockwise) both valves. Attach the tubing and flare fitting assembly as shown.

2. Fill the container with cold water to allow for submersion of the coil. Turn the valve stem of the high-pressure service valve 3 turns clockwise (midposition). Bleed the air from the tubing by slowly loosening the tubing nut at the low-pressure service valve. Test all connections for leaks.

3. Start the engine and adjust its speed to 1200 rpm. Open the car windows and move the air-conditioning operating lever to the *max* position and the blower switch to *high*.

4. Slowly turn the valve stem of the low-pressure service valve clockwise ½ turn and check the sight glass for a flow of refrigerant. After 20 minutes of operation, with liquid flowing through the

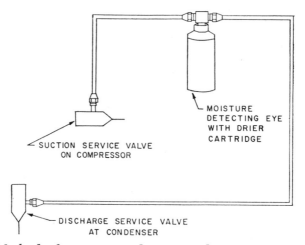

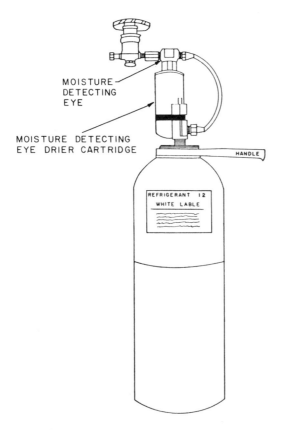

Fig. 261. Method of connecting drier cartridge into system to remove excess moisture.

MOISTURE DETECTING EYE

MOISTURE DETECTING EYE DRIER CARTRIDGE

HANDLE

REFRIGERANT 12
WHITE LABLE

Fig. 262. A drier cartridge, connected to a tank of Freon, insures that the induced charge will be free of moisture.

moisture detecting eye, the color of the dot will indicate the moisture content of the system. If the dot shows *pink,* excessive moisture is present. A *light blue* coloring is an indication that the moisture content is on the borderline and should be lowered. If the dot changes to a *dark blue,* the same color as the dot on the eye, the system is safe.

Correcting a Wet Air-Conditioning System. Make up an assembly of tubing, a 30-cubic inch drier cartridge, and the detecting eye. Hook up the assembly as follows:

1. Remove the valve stem caps from both service valves. Fully backseat (counterclockwise) both valves. Remove the caps from the valve service ports. Remove the flare plugs from the tubing and drier cartridge assembly and attach the tubing flare nuts to the service valves. Elevate the drier and cartridge assembly above compressor height to facilitate absorption.

2. Turn the valve stem of the high-pressure service valve three turns clockwise and slowly loosen the tubing nut at the low-pressure service port to bleed the air from the tubing and drier. Test all connections for leaks and correct if necessary. Turn the valve stem of the low-pressure service valve 3 turns clockwise.

3. Allow the vehicle to set for 24 hours with the drier assembly connected. When the detecting eye has turned a *deep blue,* matching the comparison color dot on the dry eye unit, the system is sufficiently dry to permit satisfactory operation.

Leak Testing the System. Whenever a leak is suspected, or a service operation performed which results in disturbing lines or connections, it is advisable to test for leaks.

The Leak Detector. The tool is a propane gas-burning torch which is used to locate a leak at any part of the Freon system. Freon gas drawn into the sampling tube attached to the torch will cause the flame to change color in proportion to the size of the leak. **CAUTION: *Do not use the lighted detector in any place where combustible or explosive gases, dusts, or vapors may be present.***

Operating the Detector:

1. Open the control valve until a low hiss of gas is heard. Then light the gas in the opening of the chimney.

2. Adjust the flame until the desired volume is obtained. This is most satisfactory when the blue flame is approximately ⅜″ above the reaction plate. The plate will heat quickly to a cherry red.

Fɪɢ. 263. Using the Allstadt electronic leak detector.

3. Explore for leaks by moving the end of the sampling hose around possible leak points in the system. Do not pinch or kink the hose. Since Freon is heavier than air, it is good practice to place the open end of the sampling hose immediately below the point being tested. CAUTION: Avoid breathing the fumes that are produced by the burning of Freon gas. Such fumes are toxic in large concentrations.

4. Watch for color changes. The color of the flame, which passes through the reaction plate, will change to *yellow* when the sampling hose draws in a very small amount of Freon. Larger leaks will be indicated by a change in color to a *vivid purplish blue*. The flame will return to its normal *pale blue* again as the hose passes the leak. **Note:** If the flame remains *yellow* when the hose is removed from

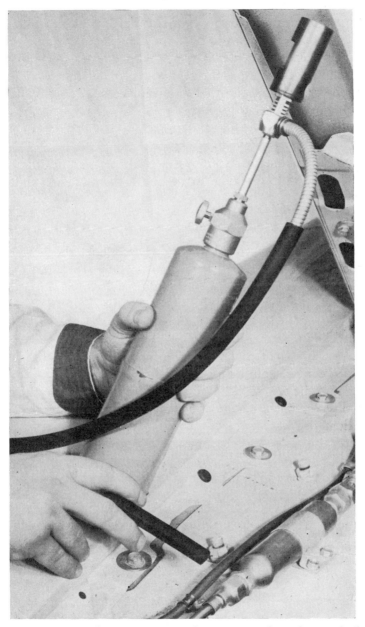

Fig. 264. Using the propane gas-burning torch to locate leaks.

the leak, the leak detector is defective. Either insufficient air is being drawn into the reaction chamber or the reaction plate is dirty.

Compressor Service. To service the compressor, it must be isolated from the system and removed from the car, except for a belt replacement or an oil level check. The only service work recommended is replacement of the clutch, the reed valve plate, the service valves, or the crankshaft oil seal; otherwise, replacement of the entire unit is recommended.

Isolating the Compressor:

1. Run the engine for 10 minutes with the system in full operation to stabilize it and to work the Freon out of the oil. Then shut off the engine.

2. Frontseat the low-pressure service valve (fully clockwise).

3. Start the engine and connect a jumper wire to operate the compressor for a five-second interval. Disconnect the jumper for a five-second interval. Repeat the cycle four times to pump the Freon from the compressor and into the condenser.

4. Shut off the engine, and then frontseat the high-pressure service valve (fully clockwise). The compressor is now ready to be removed from the car for service.

Checking the Oil Level. Each pump contains a different oil level specification which must be secured from the manufacturer's manual. Because the air-conditioning system is a sealed one, the oil does not need replacement unless it has become contaminated by metallic filings, dust, or dirt.

1. After isolating the compressor, the service valves are frontseated (fully clockwise). Check to be sure.

2. Slowly remove the oil filler plug to bleed the pressure.

3. Insert a clean black wire into the filler hole until it bottoms. It may be necessary to rotate the crankshaft to obtain clearance.

4. Remove the wire and measure the height of the oil. Compare this against specifications. Add the necessary amount of the correct grade of special refrigeration oil.

5. If this is the extent of service work to be performed, and the compressor is to be put back into service, bleed the air from the compressor crankcase by installing the filler plug loosely. Then "crack open" the low-pressure service valve to allow Freon to enter the crankcase. Being heavier than air, it forces the air up and out of the filler plug. Tighten the filler plug.

OIL FILLER HOLE OIL DIP ROD

DISCHARGE VALVE
(MAXIMUM CLOCKWISE
POSITION)

SUCTION VALVE
(MAXIMUM CLOCKWISE
POSITION)

FIG. 265. Using a piece of black wire to measure compressor oil level.

6. Backseat both service valves (fully counterclockwise) to open the system. Replace both valve stem caps.

Compressor Repair. There are a great many different kinds of compressors found in general service work. Exploded views of several of the more commonly used units are shown so that the mechanic can see just what service work is possible and how to go about it.

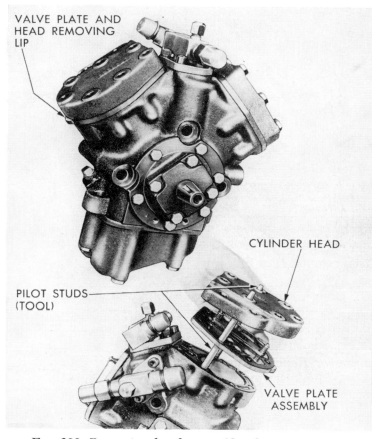

VALVE PLATE AND
HEAD REMOVING
LIP

CYLINDER HEAD

PILOT STUDS
(TOOL)

VALVE PLATE
ASSEMBLY

FIG. 266. Removing head on a Chrysler compressor.

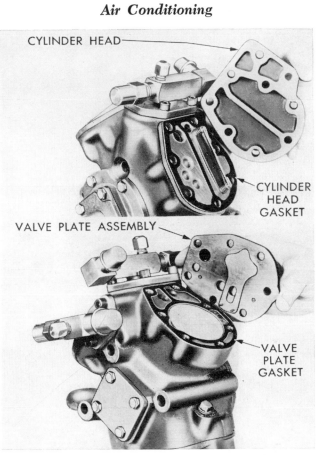

FIG. 267. Replacing cylinder head gasket.

FIG. 268. Magnetic clutch adjusting screws.

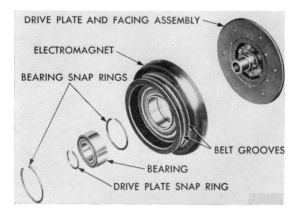

FIG. 269. Disassembled view of magnetic clutch.

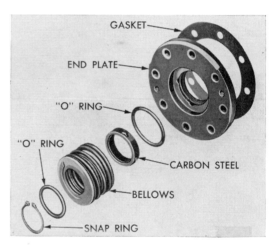

FIG. 270. Compressor oil seal details.

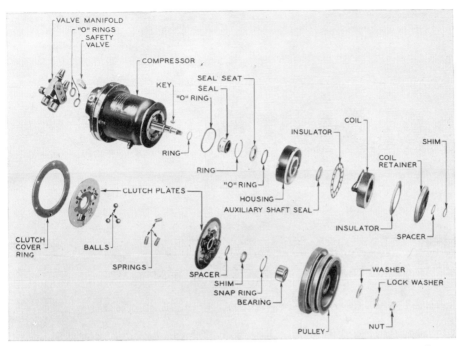

Fig. 271. Exploded view of General Motors' compressor and clutch assembly.

Fig. 272. Disassembly of clutch and pulley assembly.

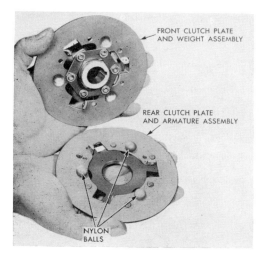

FIG. 273. Details of nylon drive balls and clutch plates.

FIG. 274. Removing clutch coil and its associated parts.

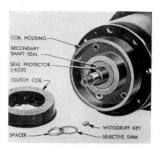

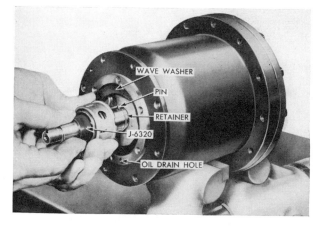

FIG. 275. Removing rotating shaft seal.

TROUBLESHOOTING

A performance test should be conducted to determine if the system is operating in a satisfactory manner. It should be used by the serviceman as a guide in diagnosing trouble.

The following fixed conditions must be adhered to in order to make it possible to compare the performance of the system being tested with the standards below:

1. Doors and windows closed.

2. Hood up.

3. Controls set for *full* outside air, blower on *HI*, COLD lever set for maximum cooling, and HEAT control must be in the *off* position.

4. Engine running at 1500 rpm.

5. Vehicle in neutral and an 18″ fan in front of the condenser radiator.

6. System "settled out" by running it for approximately 10 minutes.

7. Compressor hand shutoff valves fully counterclockwise.

8. The following performance data define normal operation of one typical system under the above conditions. The temperature-pressure spread shown indicates differences which can be expected due to humidity variations:

Ambient *Air Temperature*	*70°*	*80°*	*90°*	*100°*
Minimum discharge temperature	45°–52°	45°–54°	46°–56°	48°–60°
Maximum head pressure	140–160	145–220	190–250	210–280
Minimum suction pressure	16–22	20–28	21–31	22–35

TROUBLESHOOTING CHART

TROUBLES	CAUSES
1. Drafts	1a. Poor air outlet adjustment.
	1b. Car temperature too low due to a stuck thermostat switch.
2. Shortage of air supply at outlets	2a. Car temperature up due to improper position of controls, slipping fan, or clogged air passage through the cooling coil.
	2b. Low fan speed due to low voltage or bad bearings.
3. Water dripping into passenger compartment	3a. Drip pan or drain tubes stopped up.
	3b. Housing sweating.

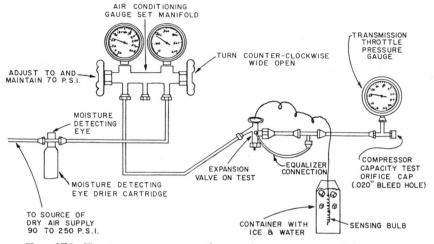

FIG. 276. Testing expansion valve with unit removed from car.

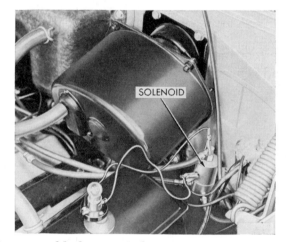

FIG. 277. Using a troubleshooting light to test operation of solenoid which operates recirculating and fresh air door controls on Chrysler products.

TROUBLESHOOTING CHART—(Continued)

TROUBLES	CAUSES
4. Hissing noise at expansion valve	4a. Shortage of refrigerant. Check the sight glass.
	4b. Restriction in the liquid line.
5. Partial frosting and sweating of the cooling unit or poor cooling	5a. Improperly adjusted controls.
	5b. Heater valve does not cut off circulation of the engine coolant through the heater core with the heat control *off*.

Fig. 278. Testing Chrysler water valve fooler circuit.

Fig. 279. Testing Chrysler water outlet lever. When lever is in *closed* position, it must rest against stop with spring loose.

TROUBLESHOOTING CHART—(Continued)

TROUBLES	CAUSES
	5c. Shortage of refrigerant.
	5d. Restricted or clogged liquid line.
	5e. Thermostat switch inoperative.
	5f. Expansion valve inoperative.
6. Failure to cool	6a. Heater valve does not cut off circulation of the engine coolant through the heater core with the HEAT control in the *off* position.
	6b. Faulty thermostat switch.
	6c. Slipping clutch.
	6d. Loss of refrigerant charge.
	6e. Blower not operating properly.

TROUBLESHOOTING CHART—(Continued)

TROUBLES	CAUSES
	6f. Insufficient air.
	6g. Stopped up liquid line or receiver-dehydrator.
	6h. Faulty expansion valve.
7. Intermittent failure to cool	7a. Freeze-up in high humidity areas which can be corrected by raising the low limit of the thermostat switch.
8. Too cool	8a. Faulty thermostat switch.
	8b. Stuck clutch.
9. High gauge reading on the high side of the system	9a. Air or excessive refrigerant in the system.
	9b. Blocked air circulation through the condenser.
	9c. High engine temperature.
10. Low gauge reading on the high side of the system	10a. Shortage of refrigerant.
	10b. Faulty compressor.
11. High gauge reading on the low side of the system	11a. Clutch slippage.
	11b. Excessively high head or side pressure.
	11c. Over-feeding of the expansion valve.
	11d. Faulty compressor.
12. Low gauge reading on the low side of the system	12a. Shortage of refrigerant.
	12b. Clutch will not disengage.
	12c. Restriction in the liquid line, suction line, receiver-dehydrator, or screen at the expansion valve.
	12d. Cooling coil dirty or iced up.

REVIEW QUESTIONS

1. What type of heater is used with an air conditioner?
2. How is air directed to the windshield defroster outlets in a hot-water type heater?
3. How is the water temperature controlled in a hot-water type heater?
4. What ignites the fuel in the gasoline-burning type of heater?
5. What inspection is recommended for the fuel nozzle and mixer assembly?
6. What are the indications of improper operation of the nozzle and mixer assembly?
7. What gap is specified for the spark plug?
8. What must be replaced along with a new vibrator?
9. What important precaution should be taken before examining the spray pattern of the fuel?

10. Why is it necessary to dehumidify the air in an air-conditioning system?
11. What part of the system acts to dehumidify the air?
12. In what two ways can heat be measured?
13. What are the two kinds of heat?
14. What is the difference between a saturated and superheated vapor?
15. What is the purpose of the expansion valve as discussed in the Theory of Operation section?
16. What is the purpose of the receiver-dehydrator?
17. What controls the expansion valve?
18. What is the purpose of the sight glass?
19. What must be done to the system before any service work is to be performed?
20. Why is it so important to observe safety precautions in handling drums of Freon?
21. What precaution is given for the discharge of Freon into the shop?
22. Why is it important to wear safety goggles when handling Freon?
23. Why is it important to open fittings slowly?
24. For what purposes is the manifold gauge set used?
25. How is the air bled from the manifold gauge set lines?
26. How can you damp out needle fluctuations of the gauges?
27. When must the system be depressurized?
28. Why must the valves be opened slowly when depressurizing the system?
29. Why must the system be evacuated?
30. What two methods are used to evacuate the system?
31. In what state must the refrigerant be when it is added to the system?
32. Why must the Freon drum be weighed when charging the system?
33. How can you tell when to stop adding Freon when making a partial charge of a system?
34. Why is it so important to test the moisture content of the system during the servicing process?
35. What is an indication of an excessive moisture content?
36. How long does the drier take to remove the moisture?
37. What are the two types of leak detectors available?
38. What precaution is given for using the leak detector?
39. What is an indication of a leak?
40. What service work can be done to the compressor?
41. How is the compressor isolated from the rest of the system?
42. Why is it necessary to establish a fixed set of conditions to judge the efficiency of a suspected air conditioning system?

INDEX BY TOPIC

Numbers in **boldface** refer to illustrations

629.27
G487

TL
275
G53